Palgrave Studies in (Re)Presenting Gender

Series Editor
Emma Rees
Director, Institute of Gender Studies
University of Chester
Chester, UK

The focus of Palgrave Studies in (Re)Presenting Gender is on gender and representation. The 'arts' in their broadest sense – TV, music, film, dance, and performance – and media re-present (where 'to represent' is taken in its literal sense of 'to present again', or 'to give back') gender globally. How this re-presentation might be understood is core to the series.

In re-presenting gendered bodies, the contributing authors can shift the spotlight to focus on marginalised individuals' negotiations of gender and identity. In this way, minority genders, subcultural genders, and gender inscribed on, in, and by queer bodies, take centre stage. When the 'self' must participate in and interact with the world through the body, how that body's gender is talked about – and side-lined or embraced by hegemonic forces – becomes paramount. These processes of representation – how cultures 'give back' gender to the individual – are at the heart of this series.

More information about this series at
http://www.palgrave.com/gp/series/16541

Francesca Sobande

The Digital Lives of Black Women in Britain

palgrave
macmillan

Francesca Sobande
School of Journalism, Media and Culture
Cardiff University
Cardiff, UK

ISSN 2662-9364   ISSN 2662-9372   (electronic)
Palgrave Studies in (Re)Presenting Gender
ISBN 978-3-030-46678-7   ISBN 978-3-030-46679-4   (eBook)
https://doi.org/10.1007/978-3-030-46679-4

© The Editor(s) (if applicable) and The Author(s), under exclusive license to Springer Nature Switzerland AG 2020
Chapters 2 and 4 are licensed under the terms of the Creative Commons Attribution 4.0 International License (http://creativecommons.org/licenses/by/4.0/). For further details see licence information in the chapters.
This work is subject to copyright. All rights are solely and exclusively licensed by the Publisher, whether the whole or part of the material is concerned, specifically the rights of translation, reprinting, reuse of illustrations, recitation, broadcasting, reproduction on microfilms or in any other physical way, and transmission or information storage and retrieval, electronic adaptation, computer software, or by similar or dissimilar methodology now known or hereafter developed.
The use of general descriptive names, registered names, trademarks, service marks, etc. in this publication does not imply, even in the absence of a specific statement, that such names are exempt from the relevant protective laws and regulations and therefore free for general use.
The publisher, the authors and the editors are safe to assume that the advice and information in this book are believed to be true and accurate at the date of publication. Neither the publisher nor the authors or the editors give a warranty, expressed or implied, with respect to the material contained herein or for any errors or omissions that may have been made. The publisher remains neutral with regard to jurisdictional claims in published maps and institutional affiliations.

Cover credit: Francesca Sobande

This Palgrave Macmillan imprint is published by the registered company Springer Nature Switzerland AG
The registered company address is: Gewerbestrasse 11, 6330 Cham, Switzerland

To all who are (and were) (t)here.

ACKNOWLEDGEMENTS

This book is derived in part from my article, Sobande, Francesca. (2017). 'Watching me watching you: Black women in Britain on YouTube.' Published in *European Journal of Cultural Studies* 20(6): 655–671, available online: https://doi.org/10.1177/1367549417733001.

This book is derived in part from my doctoral thesis, Sobande, Francesca. (2018). 'Digital diaspora and (re)mediating Black women in Britain.' *Student thesis: Doctoral Thesis › Doctor of Philosophy* University of Dundee.

This book is derived in part from my co-authored article, Sobande, Francesca, Fearfull, Anne & Brownlie, Douglas. (2019). 'Resisting media marginalisation: Black women's digital content and collectivity.' Published in *Consumption Markets & Culture*, 29 January 2019, © Taylor & Francis, available online: https://www.tandfonline.com/doi/10.1080/10253866.2019.1571491.

Thanks to the School of Journalism, Media and Culture at Cardiff University for funds towards making portions of this book open access.

CONTENTS

1 **Why the Digital Lives of Black Women in Britain?**   1
   Digital Diasporic Dynamics: Transnational, National,
   and Regional Relations   4
   Different Experiences of Black Life   9
   Where I Write From   12
   What Follows   15
   References   20

2 **Black Women and the Media in Britain**   29
   Self-Representing and Organising Around Black Women
   and the Media   31
   The Politics of Representation   37
   Conceptualising Black Women's Media Representation
   and Experiences   43
   Representations of Black Women on Television   45
   Regionality and Rurality   52
   Concluding Thoughts   54
   References   55

3 **Black Women's Digital, Creative, and Cultural Industry Experiences**   65
   (Un)defining Work, Labour, and the Marketplace   67

*Digital Developments, Media, and the Creative
and Cultural Industries* 70
Carving Out (Y)our Own Spaces and Narratives 72
*Navigating Different Digital Experiences and the Prospect
of Corporate Co-optation* 73
Spectacularisation and Superficiality 78
*Social Media Terms of Service, Shadowbanning,
and Surveillance* 83
Harassment, Bullying, and Abuse 85
Concluding Thoughts 89
References 91

4 **Black Women's Digital Diaspora, Collectivity,
and Resistance** 101
Digital Blackness, Borders, and a Politics of Difference 103
Black Digital Dialogue Between Britain and the US 105
Black Women's Natural Hair Vlogs and Knowledge-Sharing 110
(Medi)activist Sentiments 117
Concluding Thoughts 121
References 123

5 **(Un)Defining the Digital Lives of Black Women
in Britain** 131
References 140

Index 145

CHAPTER 1

Why the Digital Lives of Black Women in Britain?

Abstract This chapter outlines questions that buttress this work, such as: How is digital media implicated in the lives of Black women in Britain? In what ways do such digital experiences involve forms of creativity and cultural production? How are the intersections of anti-Black racism, sexism, and capitalism connected to this? What is the 'digital' in the lives of Black women in Britain, and how can it be both a source of joy and pain? How and why are Black women often identified as digital 'trendsetters', while being both erased and hyper-visible as creators, knowledge-producers, and social movement builders? This chapter provides an overview of key themes in this book, including digital diasporic dynamics and transnational, national, and regional relations.

Keywords Black girls · Black women · Childhood · Diaspora · Digital · Social media

How is digital media implicated in the lives of Black women in Britain? In what ways do such digital experiences involve forms of creativity and cultural production? How are the intersections of anti-Black racism, sexism, and capitalism connected to this? What is the 'digital' in the lives of Black women in Britain, and how can it be both a source of joy and pain? How and why are Black women often identified as digital 'trendsetters', while being both erased and hyper-visible as creators, knowledge-producers, and social movement builders? These questions buttress *The Digital Lives of Black Women in Britain*—a book which focuses on issues, experiences, and perspectives that are seldom addressed in media, cultural, and digital studies.

This work is predominantly based on my research which commenced in 2015, but its roots developed prior to the rise of content-sharing sites and social media such as Facebook, Instagram, Twitter, TikTok and YouTube. Since childhood, my mind has homed a patchwork of thoughts on Black people's depiction on-screen and their involvement in the creation of media. I have memories of North American media imports and television shows from Britain—*Comin' Atcha!, Bump 'N' Grind, The Fresh Prince of Bel-Air, Kerching!, Harry and Cosh, Moesha, Desmond's, My Wife and Kids, EastEnders, 3 Non-Blondes, One on One, Cutting It, Hollyoaks, Waterloo Road, The Crust, Hang Time, Girlfriends, The Story of Tracy Beaker, Sister, Sister*…the list goes on.

I watched a lot of TV—I still do, but now mostly online. Often glibly dubbed 'urban TV', the channel Trouble was a staple part of my childhood television diet because it offered a broader range of depictions of Black lives than those (un)available through most mainstream media outlets in Britain. As I got older, my pre-teen television musings morphed into meaning-making sparked by different expressions and experiences of Black digital diasporic culture (Everett 2009), as well as my understanding of how Black women in Britain have come together throughout history 'to record *our* version of events' (Bryan et al. 2018, p. 1).

Just as the development of television 'altered our world' (Williams 2003, p. 3), so too did the rise of the internet and Wi-Fi connections from the 1990s onwards (McIlwain 2020; Roberts 2019), paired with the popularity of mobile devices which enabled some people to create and communicate online and while on the move. Simple and sturdy mobile phones that were likened to indestructible bricks were gradually crowded out by slicker models with online functions and aesthetic appeal. Screen time was no longer just about the prospect of being at the cinema, in front of a television, or a desktop computer. Instead, it now included the possibility of time spent with friends crowded around one person's mobile screen and connecting to the internet—possibly at an exorbitant cost—without needing to physically plug in a device.

I passed time on websites such as DressUpGames, Piczo, and Dollz-Mania. I created amusingly bad polyphonic ringtones, marveled at the magnetism of Comic Sans, and made my way through Nintendo 64, Game Boy Advance, and PlayStation games—including gems from the Crash Bandicoot, Pokémon, Sims, and Tony Hawk series. Eventually, I moved on to mining Xanga for the latest 'noughties' emo and post-hardcore music demos, in-between wistfully browsing Fueled by Ramen band merchandise when Fall Out Boy had just started to grace the cover of *Kerrang!* magazine.

During my childhood, the nuances of the different digital experiences of Black girls and Black women in Britain were far from being at the forefront of my mind. This is not to suggest that I was ever oblivious to the particularities of my identity as a Black (and 'mixed-race'[1]) girl in a predominantly white society. Rather, as a child exploring the internet, I was not preoccupied with considering connections between people's digital experiences and their racial and gender identities. Later in life, this shifted.

Since embarking on my research project, the motivation behind writing this book has not changed, including frustration at how Black women's media experiences and creative and cultural contributions are often structurally dismissed and obstructed. I seek to reflect on the contemporary media experiences of Black women in Britain, especially those connected to internet activity—from enjoyable and enriching online encounters, to participating in digital forms of cultural production and contending with online harassment and abuse. If it is true that '[n]othing seems to escape capital's control, whether affects, emotions and feelings, linguistic skills, or manifestations of desire, dreams or thought' (Mbembe 2019, p. 43), then efforts to understand the digital experiences of Black women in Britain must reckon with how capitalist frameworks impact them. Consequently, I write these words with the aim of contributing to dialogue about the relationship between anti-Black racism, sexism, capitalism, media, the internet, and the lives of Black women of African descent[2] in Britain.

Despite the relatively unchanging nature of the reasons for me doing this work, over the last decade media depictions and the digital experiences of Black women in Britain *have* changed, at least, to some extent (Adewunmi 2012; Amoah 2019; Gabriel 2016; Sobande 2017; Sobande et al. 2019; Wilson-Ojo 2017). Yet, the digital experiences of Black women in Britain are scarcely considered in scholarship (t)here, including media, cultural, and digital studies. Black people are often excluded—both literally and conceptually—from academia in Britain, in addition to many different institutional and educational environments (Johnson et al. 2018; Johnson 2019). Thus, *The Digital Lives of Black Women in Britain* was written against a societal backdrop punctuated by the structural omission and oppression of Black people (t)here, and impacted by the interlocking nature of anti-Black racism, sexism, classism, and other forms of discrimination (Bryan et al. 2018; Crenshaw 1989, 2017; Hill Collins 2000; Lewis 1993).

This book considers how media is implicated in Black women's lives in Britain—ranging from accounts of twentieth-century activism and television representations, to experiences of YouTube, Twitter, and the internet. Drawing on Black feminist approaches, I synthesise critical understandings of digital culture, gender, race, Blackness, and Britain, to offer a text that dances between disciplinary boundaries and focuses on the lives of Black women. In doing so, this work critically contributes to media, cultural, and digital studies, particularly in Britain. Perhaps, it generatively disrupts these research fields and how matters to do with Black lives, anti-Blackness, and, specifically, Black women in Britain, are rarely addressed.

While the focus of my book is the digital lives of Black women in Britain, when addressing associated issues I affirm that digital encounters, embodied experiences, and material conditions are inherently entwined. Can lives ever *be* 'digital'? What does, or can, the concept of 'digital lives' even mean, resemble and feel like? Any professed clean-cut distinction between online and offline 'worlds' and 'lives' is always a blurred and illusionary one, at best (Daniels et al. 2017; Emejulu and McGregor 2016; Kolko et al. 2000; Nakamura 2008). For this reason, my book does not merely focus on the online experiences of Black women in Britain. More precisely, it accounts for how digital content creation, humorous exchanges, marketplace interactions, meaning-making, and collectivity, takes shape in relation to different types of technology and digital space—in addition to so-called 'in real life' (IRL) contexts and cultures.

Digital Diasporic Dynamics: Transnational, National, and Regional Relations

Significant scholarship in the early twenty-first century on African-American experiences in cyberspace illuminates that—at that time—although 'the virtual Black community' (Alkalimat 2004, p. 4) had an increasingly vibrant online presence, it was still 'in infancy barely taking baby steps' (ibid.). Since such crucial work regarding the digital experiences of Black people in the US, including communication studies scholar Catherine R. Squires' (2009) research on *African Americans and the Media*, global Black digital activity has continued to develop in dynamic ways which is explored in relation to Britain in the rigorous research of emerging scholars Rianna Walcott at King's College London and Keisha Bruce at the University of Nottingham.

Bruce (forthcoming, 2022) examines 'the creation, circulation, and engagement with Black women's digital visual culture'. Her work demonstrates how 'digital diasporic identity and community is created and performed on social media through processes of visuality and affect' (Bruce, forthcoming, 2022). Relatedly, Walcott's research (forthcoming, 2021) examines 'how language is disseminated between geographically and culturally disparate people who self-identify as Black, and how linguistic acts of performative identity that Black British women use contribute to the articulation of a group Black identity through shared language and experience'.

In November 2018, Keisha Bruce (@keishastweets) used Twitter to call for expressions of interest in putting together a panel on digital Blackness for the American Studies Association (ASA) 2019 Annual Meeting which took place in Honolulu, Hawai'i. Rianna Walcott (@rianna_walcott) and I (@chess_ess) responded. This led to the three of us corresponding for months at a distance online to create our panel—'Navigating Transnational Digital Blackness: Networked Publics and Decolonized Ethnographic Approaches'—chaired by African American studies and English scholar Cynthia A. Young. We drew on paramount work on media, culture, digital and communication studies, and Black people's online experiences in the US (Benjamin 2019; Brock 2018, 2020; Clark 2014; Everett 2009; Gray 2015; Jackson 2016; McMillan Cottom 2017; Noble 2018; Noble and Tynes 2016; Steele 2016a, 2016b, 2017), while focusing on the specifics of Black lives in Britain.

Our ASA session continued conversations that Walcott and I took part in at a panel in 2018 on 'Bridges and Boundaries: Black (British) Digital Discourses'—chaired by communication studies scholar Jessica H. Lu. Walcott and I co-organised the panel to participate in Intentionally Digital, Intentionally Black—the first national conference of the African American History, Culture, and Digital Humanities (AADHum) Initiative at the University of Maryland. We did this together with layla-roxanne hill who is a curator, artist, and organiser who advocates for non-commodifiable collective liberation, and Melz Owusu who is a non-binary, decolonial and Black feminist thinker, a community activist, and is undertaking a PhD at the University of Cambridge—exploring the relationship between epistemic and social justice.

In sum, the scholarship of Walcott and Bruce is critically contributing to the development and direction of Black digital studies in Britain. In addition, the work of both Owusu and hill significantly shapes various movements for radical liberation on multiple fronts. Individually, we each explore different landscapes, experiences, understandings, and expressions of Black life across a range of digital spaces and offline places. Collectively, we work towards making a critical intervention concerning the erasure and articulation of Black diasporic experiences, knowledge, and cultural production—particularly in relation to the specifics of being Black in Britain, in various regions.

As is suggested by film and media studies scholar Anna Everett's (2009) innovative research on race and cyberspace, the term 'digital diaspora' can be a useful one to refer to the myriad examples of how Black people around the world have connected, communicated, and created space(s) by using different digital technologies, platforms, and prowess. Black digital diasporic dialogue, including social media discussions between Black people, can facilitate the feeling that such online communication overcomes and erodes geographical borders—despite persistent barriers to the free movement of Black people within and beyond countries and digital enclaves. Put briefly, digital spaces can enable Black people in different places to communicate with each other and come together, even momentarily, and as part of 'the online Black public sphere' (Steele 2016a, p. 2) which among many other experiences can involve collectivity, creativity, relationality, joy and resistance (Clark 2014; Gabriel 2016; Lu and Steele 2019; Sobande et al. 2019; Steele 2016a, 2016b, 2017).

Still, social constructions of the nation-state, citizenship, ethnicity, racial identity and borders (hill 2018; Omonira-Oyekanmi 2010; Otele 2017)—which can be 'those places where, for many of our contemporaries, the world comes undone and globalization comes up against its limits' (Mbembe 2019, p. 22)—impact digital experiences irrespective of feelings of borderlessness. Also, '[i]dentity formation, the sense of being an embodied, located individual, does not occur in isolation from within a mono-logic of cultural development and formation' (Young 2000, p. 45).

Therefore, focusing on the digital lives of Black women in Britain involves thinking about how such lives are connected to and disconnected from those of Black women in other countries.

My work considers how issues related to regionality factor into the lives of Black women in Britain (hill and Sobande 2018; Sulter 1986), both online and offline. I remain skeptical of the adequacy and specificity of describing someone or something as being located 'in Britain'—because, where exactly? My perspective relates to an awareness of how claims of Britain's unified nature are often effectively and ardently contested, and how stark differences between life in nations within Britain—England, Northern Ireland, Scotland, and Wales—are often ignored as part of sweeping statements about life (t)here.

In turn, and given 'the value of cultural specificity in understanding emerging media' (Florini 2019, p. 5), throughout my book I consider how different regions where Black women are based affect their media experiences and lives in certain ways (Kay 2010; Palma 2017; The Afro-Caribbean Women's Association 1990). Even so, I do refer to the lives of Black women as being 'in Britain'—while clarifying different regional experiences—but without specific reference to being 'British'. My avoidance of the term 'British', unless used when referring to the chosen words of others, is partly based on recognition of 'widespread ambivalence among some Black people about identifying themselves as *British*, in any unadorned, unembellished or unhyphenated sense' (Chambers 2017, p. xvii).

My position is shaped by Jacqueline Nassy Brown's (1998) anthropological research related to 'why and how black identity is constituted as the mutual opposite of English and British identities' (p. 291). Additionally, given that the concept of Britishness is often equated with experiences in England, with little to no connection to those in Northern Ireland, Scotland, and Wales, I choose to observe differences between the notion of being British and being in Britain. My decision to avoid a focus on the term 'British' is not intended to be dismissive of the identities and experiences of individuals who refer to themselves as such or are identified this way by others. Instead, this decision is aligned with my intention to avoid the exclusionary nationalistic sentiments that can be associated with Britishness.

What's more, I aim to eschew undermining the different national and regional-specific ways that Black women in Britain may identify or be identified as—including English, Scottish, Welsh, and Northern Irish

(British Social Attitudes 2013; Northern Ireland Statistics and Research Agency 2013a). I also intend to avoid negating the experiences of Black women in Britain who primarily identify with a sense of nationhood located outside of Britain, as well as the experiences of those who do not identify with any notion of nationhood or citizenship—including a 'transactional model of citizenship' (Benjamin 2019, p. 19) which 'presumes that people's primary value hinges on the ability to spend money and, in the digital age, expend attention … browsing, clicking, buying' (ibid.).

To be Black in Britain can distinctly differ to being Black elsewhere. Further still, to be Black in a capital city may be to experience life in a way that contrasts with the realities of Black people living in rural settings. Still, there can be commonalities between Black diasporic experiences (Emejulu and Sobande 2019; Figueroa-Vásquez 2020; Florvil and Plumly 2018; Palmer 2011, 2016; Perlow et al. 2018; Sims and Njaka 2019; Twine 2004, 2010). In my work, the term 'diaspora' encompasses felt, yet, intangible and sometimes fragile connections and forms of consciousness—which along with being associated with a racialised embodied identity, ancestry, and perceived country of 'origin', are linked to (re)imagined and (re)presented notions of home and belonging.

Then again, I use the term 'diaspora' with a critical perspective of its potential to flatten distinctly different experiences (e.g. of migration, asylum-seeking, class, colourism, sexuality, gender, and religion) between Black people who are sometimes mistakenly thought to share a somewhat fixed and completely collective experience. In the words of sociologist Frederick F. Wherry (2012, p. 7):

> Just as people are born into a culture with a language and a structure of language that existed before they were born, so too do individuals find themselves by birth or by migration to inhabit a shared sense about how the world is ordered (or at least about how things ought to be ordered and done).

An example of shared struggle is navigation of the pervasive global force of white supremacy and systemic oppression faced by Black people (Gilroy 1987; Taylor 2016; Wekker 2016; Yancy 2018). Nevertheless, existence of any type of such shared struggle does not disprove differences between Black people and does not solely define what it means to be Black.

Different Experiences of Black Life

Due to systemic factors such as colourism which involves the structural favouring of light-skinned people and the contrastingly severe oppression and dehumanisation of people who are darker-skinned (Adegoke 2019; Amoah 2019; Gabriel 2007; Tate 2009, 2017a, 2017b)—including within Black communities—not all Black people are equally subjected to forms of anti-Blackness. Given the rifeness of white supremacy, coupled with their perceived embodied proximity to whiteness, light-skinned Black people—including those also identified as 'mixed-race'—can contribute to, and, be complicit in, anti-Blackness and colourism. Accordingly, when reflecting on the digital lives of Black women in Britain it is necessary to tarry with how Black women's many experiences are sculpted by different types of interlocking structural oppression (Crenshaw 1989, 2017; Hill Collins 2000), such as anti-Blackness, sexism, and 'the impact of colorism (also referred to as shadeism)' (Amoah 2019, p. 1).

I consider how digital spaces shape the identities, self-expression, and lives of Black women in Britain, and how Black women in Britain shape digital spaces, and environments beyond, but, connected to them. In agreement with the perspective of curator and writer Erika Dalya Muhammad (2001), throughout my book '"digital space" is used as a deliberately elastic term to define both old-school and new-school media practices that respond to continual technological innovation' (p. 92). One Black woman's digital source of joy and refuge may be another's source of stress and struggle. My book wrestles with tensions between Black women's creation of online content sometimes being a labour of love, a form of (un)credited labour or, simply, an entertaining and enjoyable pastime.

In this context, what does 'labour' mean? When is it present or absent? How is it claimed and (un)compensated? When considering these questions in the chapters that follow there is acknowledgement of the intricacies of online commentaries which can circulate in an arguably transnational Black digital diaspora (Everett 2009; Sobande et al. 2019). As part of such discussion there is also recognition of how Black digital diasporic spaces can be ones where a sense of community and kinship may feel as though it exists, alongside hierarchical relations and hegemonic discourse influenced by the domination of the English language (Emejulu and Sobande 2019).

Research and writing about perceived 'minoritarian users and makers of digital culture' (De Kosnik and Feldman 2019, p. 2) points to how people's identities and social relations are continually (re)produced as part of their engagement with on-screen images and media practices at different stages of their lives. My book involves contemplation concerning some of the experiences of Black girls—including constant oppressive scrutiny that they face (Dawes 2012; Halliday 2019; Okanlawon 2019)—and how media depictions they encounter as children can influence them, even in later life. I discuss how some 'parents construct Black children's engagement with media as being a counter-cultural coping mechanism, to temper the potential racial and diasporic discordance of their children's identities' (Sobande 2018, p. 37) in predominantly white societies.

Such parental management of children's media is by no means exclusive to the twenty-first century, but the development of digital media and technology has affected how parents may attempt to manage and mediate the consumer culture experiences of their Black children, and by extension, their self-perceptions. Informed by extant studies, I use the words 'consumer culture' in reference to 'the intensification of consumerism along with increasing prominence of consumption as social, cultural and economic activity that has come about with free-market capitalism and that is characteristic of late modernity, or what many refer to as postmodernity' (Kravets et al. 2018, p. 1). Influenced by critical studies of consumer culture, this book responds to recent calls for more research on the racial and racist dynamics of media and marketplace activity to further develop understandings of how racialised subjectivities and racist interactions are experienced online and around the world (Grier et al. 2019; Lindridge et al. 2015).

Social media and online content-sharing platforms are key sites of consumer culture, as well as sites of contemporary meaning-making, including as part of recent 'conversations about race and racial inequality' (Anderson and Hitlin 2016, p. 2)—especially those led by Black people (Clark 2014), who have made use of networked forms of communication in ingenious ways for centuries (Brock 2020). Since the 1990s, 'black connectivity online seems to have achieved a critical mass' (Everett 2009, p. 10) and contributed to the formation of national and global solidarities and social movements (McIlwain 2020; Taylor 2016). Despite this, there is a relative dearth of in-depth empirical research which focuses on how the production and spectatorship of digital media and content is intertwined with issues concerning race, ethnicity, gender and, specifically,

Black life in Britain. Be that as it may, the distinct paucity of academic journal articles and books on the digital experiences of Black women in Britain should not be mistaken for an absence of Black women in Britain recording, working on, writing about and ruminating on related issues—including online.

The rise of social media and content-sharing platforms 'which contribute to many people's daily routines, has significantly affected contemporary British politics and public life' (Sobande 2019a, p. 152) in ways that Black women are highly attuned to. Ergo, as I processed the (un)expected results of the General Election in Britain in December 2019, typically, it was the critical analysis of other Black women online that I turned to for incisive accounts of the history and trajectory of Britain's political and social life. Moreover, as people and places around the world responded to the (un)anticipated COVID-19 (coronavirus) pandemic in 2020, which resulted in forms of government-directed 'lockdown' and physical distancing between people, I often attempted to make sense of what was—and was not—happening, through online conversations with Black women across a range of platforms and devices.

Black women in Britain are using digital media and spaces creatively, enabling the co-production, sharing, and documentation of knowledge in ways hardly ever afforded to them in many formal and institutional educational and academic settings. Decades have passed since leading Black feminist activist, psychosocial studies scholar, and psychotherapist Gail Lewis (cited in the Brixton Black Women's Group and the Organisation for Women of African and Asian Descent 2017) poignantly wrote about 'a time when we, as Black people, were particularly vocal, both in Britain and in the US, in expressing the need for the learning and writing of our own history, literature being central, particularly resistance literature' (pp. 2–3). Yet, many Black women today continue to strive in the same ways and for some of the same reasons, including pursuit of 'decolonisation of the mind' (ibid.)—and sometimes—with the use of digital tools.

The 2018 republication of *The Heart of The Race: Black Women's Lives in Britain* by writers, educators, activists, and scholars Beverley Bryan et al. (1985) marked a key moment in Black women's herstoricising and sustained archiving of their experiences (Akpan 2019). In the words of artist, photographer, writer, and curator Maud Sulter (1986), who penned thoughts about the book the first time it was published, *The Heart of The Race: Black Women's Lives in Britain* offered 'us the opportunity to take up the pen and document our histories for ourselves' (p. 29).

Writing about Black women's lives in Britain today is built upon the work and knowledge of Black women in previous decades; including observation of how Black women's agency is often overlooked, as 'we are usually portrayed as the passive victims of an historical necessity which began on the "dark continent" with the Slave Trade and eventually brought us to the inner-cities of the "Mother Country"' (Bryan et al. 2018, p. 2). The creativity, activism, and scholarship of those such as Bryan et al. (1985), among others, undoubtedly paved the way for current and future writing on the lives of Black women in Britain.

Black women around the world are addressing issues related to digital media and technology which are pertinent to Black people and society—elucidating the digital dynamics of democracy and politics in Kenya (Nyabola 2018), reflecting on online activism that foregrounds marginalised voices in Ghana (Mohammed 2019), writing about the lives of Black women in France (Diallo 2017; Mwasi Collectif 2019), researching power relations linked to race and technology (Benjamin 2019), examining the oppressive nature of algorithms and racist content generated by internet search results (Noble 2018), and exploring the political potential of aesthetics (Osei 2019; Sobande and Osei 2020). Resultingly, the chapters of my book are rooted in the insights of Black women—past and present.

Where I Write From

In some ways, my book is influenced by me being born and having grown up in Scotland, residing in England when starting this book, and now living in Wales. I do not disclose these details to caveat anything included in this book or to fetishise the self-disclosure and personal essay writing of Black women. Instead, I reflect on the place(s) from where I view, write about, and experience some of the issues covered in subsequent chapters as part of my efforts to articulate elements of the different lives of Black women in Britain.

I recognise potential benefits and limitations of work such as mine. It may broaden understandings of the digital experiences and lives of Black women in Britain but can never convey the richness and varied nature of all of them. I reject the idea that any one person or perspective can encompass what it means to be a Black woman in Britain today. In writing this book I do not claim to write on behalf of all Black women in Britain or to produce an exhaustive list of Black women's digital, creative, and cultural contributions. However, 'the burden of representation' (Mercer 1990, p. 61) can loom large for a Black person in Britain, where the population of Black people is less than 5% of the total population of England and Wales (Gov.uk 2018), is approximately 1% of the total population of Scotland (National Records of Scotland 2018), and is approximately 0.2% of the total population of Northern Ireland (Northern Ireland Statistics and Research Agency 2013b).

My book draws upon Black feminist and women's studies scholar Jacqueline Bobo's (2001, p. xv) vital writing on how 'Black women have confronted institutional and societal barriers in their daily lives and in their creative spaces'. Work that considerably influences mine also includes the leading research of communication, gender, and women's studies scholar Kishonna L. Gray (2015) on Black cyberfeminism—which 'as an extension of virtual feminisms and Black feminist thought, incorporates the tenets of interconnected identities, interconnected social forces, and distinct circumstances to better theorize women operating within Internet technologies and to capture the uniqueness of marginalized women' (p. 176).

Gray's (2015) Black cyberfeminist framework accounts for both the liberatory and limiting potentials of digital technology, especially as experienced, understood, and developed by Black women. As is outlined in the crucial work of sociologist and writer Tressie McMillan Cottom (2017), Black cyberfeminism can 'interrogate how social relations of dominance are translated through digitally mediated relationships with technology, the interests that produce it, and the processes that resist them' (p. 217). For these reasons and more, Black cyberfeminism (Gray 2015; McMillan Cottom 2017) orients much of my work.

At the crux of my research is an interest in the inseparability of many digital, material, and embodied experiences, along with an awareness of how hierarchical power relations are homed in digital spaces and made manifest in the development and use of digital technologies (Emejulu and McGregor 2016; Gregory 2017). Overall, my work is inspired by contributions from a range of what tend to be referred to as disciplines, fields, and subject areas. These include, but are not limited to, sociology, media and cultural studies, Black feminist studies, communication and information studies, visual studies, digital studies, and critical marketing and advertising studies which recognise that '[t]he marketplace is not simply a place where money is made; it is a site of service, a place where crusades and social movements attempt to overturn "bad'" practices' (Wherry 2012, p. 9). My work is also moulded by my participation in ongoing collective-oriented activities which foster critical discussion and actions in response to matters concerning Black lives, digital media, and marketplace settings (Johnson et al. 2019).

As well as being the outcome of over five years of research, *The Digital Lives of Black Women in Britain* is born of a kaleidoscope of conversations with friends, family, and loved ones. Although my book does not specifically focus on Black feminism and Black activism, it is nurtured by the writing and work of Black feminists and activists, such as Olive Gallimore, Gail Lewis, Melba Wilson, and individuals involved in the Brixton Black Women's Group which was founded in 1973 and created space 'to look at the questions of colonialism and the nature of capitalist society, African history and these sort of things' (Lewis cited in the Brixton Black Women's Group and the Organisation for Women of African and Asian Descent 2017, p. 1).

While my book outlines some of the ways that the digital experiences of Black women in Britain are mobilised by consciousness-raising and political intentions, it also addresses the fact that this is not the case for all. Regardless of differences between what Black women in Britain write, post about, enjoy and do online, one common component of such digital experiences is dealing with harassment (Akiwowo 2018; Allman 2019). Such harassment is often underpinned by co-dependent anti-Black racism and misogyny—namely, misogynoir, which is a term introduced in 2008 by Moya Bailey who is the digital alchemist for the Octavia E. Butler Legacy Network, and whose work focuses on how race, gender, and sexuality are represented in media and medicine.

Bailey, who curates the #transformDH Tumblr initiative in digital humanities, and whose scholarship and work has played a pivotal role in critical digital humanities developments, has written about misogynoir online since 2010 (Bailey 2010). Since then, the term 'misogynoir' has been developed and discussed in detail by Bailey, as well as Trudy who is an artist who works as an indie creator, author, writer, photographer, curator and social critic, and is the creator of Gradient Lair—a digital space about Black women, art, media, social media, sociopolitics, and culture (Bailey and Trudy 2018, pp. 767–768). Taking heed of such work and how misogynoir and intersecting oppressions impact the lives of Black women, one of several key topics of discussion in my book is how

Black women in Britain try to navigate negative aspects of their digital experiences, such as the reality of online abuse and constant exposure to traumatic content and malicious messages that are directed at them.

What Follows

The themes at the centre of my book originate from 26 in-depth interviews with Black women in Britain (aged 19–47 years old), as well as interpretive analysis of resources accessed at the Black Cultural Archives (BCA) in Brixton in London, at the British Library, and at Glasgow Women's Library (GWL). Some of the interviews occurred at cafés, over the phone or via a video call, and in other cases, they took place at the person's home. Although the chapters that follow do not include excerpts from all 26 interviews, many of the excerpts that feature encompass and echo perspectives that were expressed across most of them.

Aligned with Black feminist principles which inform my work, the methodological approach that underpins it foregrounds the experiences and knowledge of Black women in Britain, as expressed in their own words—including in interviews with me and in pre-existing written texts. Some people may think it is counterintuitive to not prioritise digital methods when researching digital encounters and activity. But, to return to previous words of mine in this chapter, I affirm that digital encounters, embodied experiences, and material conditions are inherently entwined.

I recognise researchers' 'dual charge to experiment with and work through new digital tools, but not take the tools so seriously that we lose sight of the very social conditions that have given rise to them' (Gregory 2017, p. 4). In view of that, when approaching the research that led to my book, I sought to focus on the individual lives of Black women in Britain and the material and social conditions that impact them, as a prelude to understanding their experiences of digital space, media, and technology. I did not solely want to learn about how other Black women in Britain are creating and making use of digital media. Instead, I wanted to do work that involves acknowledging, understanding, and responding to Black women's thoughts and feelings concerning such experiences, the contexts they occur within, and the lives that they are a part of—discussed with them in a setting of their choice. In other words, I principally based my book on what arose during in-depth interviews with Black women which relate to how their individual biographies (dis)connect to and from their digital experiences, as well as their shared and different herstories.

As most of the women (19) who were interviewed were in their twenties or younger, my book mainly focuses on the experiences of Black women who are part of a generation of people who are typically assumed to be very familiar with digital technology and online communication processes. All interview excerpts are attributed to pseudonyms that those who I spoke to selected for themselves. Despite my work foregrounding the thoughts and encounters of individuals who do not identify as online influencers or internet famous, there is acknowledgement of how differing levels of visibility can impact the digital experiences of Black women in Britain. After all, there are numerous examples of Black women in Britain using their digital presence and influence in creative, educational, community-oriented, and resistant ways, as well as those who focus on commercial, branding, and business opportunities (Wilson-Ojo 2017).

Throughout these pages I use the terms 'mainstream media' and 'mass-media' to refer to high-profile and longstanding corporate media organisations, outlets, and the content that they distribute (Sobande 2019b). I also understand the contestable qualities of these concepts 'given that online content produced by non-media and non-marketing professionals is continually incorporated into prominent media and marketing endeavours' (Sobande et al. 2019, p. 3). My use of the word 'spectator' is based on an understanding of the spectacular(ised) attributes of much media, as well as the active approach to watching, engaging with, and responding to it, which can be part of some people's media viewing experiences.

The connected concept of the 'gaze' can bring up various connotations (Berger 2008) such as the lingering eyes of onlookers, who watch admiringly or with intent, and can be associated with a sense of scrutiny and surveillance that Black people are structurally subjected to (Browne 2015). My perspective of a gaze affirms the notion that such a form of looking is purposeful and involves people situating themselves in relation to who or what they gaze upon. The sustained intentionality at the root of someone casting their gaze upon something or letting it linger is markedly different to the ambivalence that may be associated with a cursory glance or glimpse.

My use of the word 'practices' in relation to digital and media activities encompasses experiences which involve a habitual element and are influenced by socio-cultural norms and the broader geo-cultural locations that people find themselves in. The phrase 'digital media practices' is used in reference to commonplace digital activities, including those which are particular to the lives of some Black women in Britain. In the context of this work the term 'practices' also implies that such experiences are connected to collective sentiments and cultural conventions that are reinforced via certain institutional and social processes. Related discussion of digital remix culture concerns 'how people (re)use and (re)create digital content and commentary' (Sobande 2019a, p. 153), including as part of digital processes and practices that 'can involve editing or adding to existing visual, audio and textual content to (re)produce something new, which is tailored to capturing specific socio-cultural views and events' (ibid.).

Lastly, my perspective of the term race is based on the position that 'the socially constructed nature of race *doesn't* mean that our understanding of race and racial categories isn't somehow real or that it doesn't have real effects: quite the contrary, those categories *do* exist and they have tangible (and all too often deadly) effects on the ways that people are able to live their lives' (Kolko et al. 2000, p. 2). My understanding of how race functions also echoes the explanation offered by Erika Dalya Muhammad (2001), who curated the Race in Digital Space exhibition for the MIT List Visual Arts Center in Cambridge, Massachusetts, from 27 April to 1 July 2001, '[t]he word "race", at once positional and relational, reflects a variety of cultural realities' (p. 92).

The exhibition—Race in Digital Space—curated by Dalya Muhammad (2001) sought to 'contextualize race as a dynamic power system that is further manipulated and complicated by hi-tech devices and evolving historical paradigms' (p. 92), while also accounting for some of 'the effects of new media on the dynamics of cultural hegemony' and 'cultural interchange' (ibid.). In a similar vein, my book is intended to contextualise how power relations, digital technologies, and space impact experiences, expressions, and understandings of Black women's lives in Britain.

When closely observing media and 'consumption and market activities, the tangibility, reality and brutality of racial dynamics are almost impossible to miss' (Grier et al. 2019, p. 91). Despite perceptions of the democratised nature of digital media production processes, social media and content-sharing platforms such as YouTube and Twitter still reflect and perpetuate intersecting inequalities (Noble and Tynes 2016)—including those connected to how 'power relations of racism and sexism gain meaning in relation to one another' (Hill Collins and Bilge 2016, p. 27). Social media contexts have been identified as digital spaces that can be used to harvest and propagate far right and white supremacist politics (Daniels 2009, 2012, 2017; Lewis 2018). Therefore, while my work includes acknowledgement of the potential for digital environments to contribute to the lives and wellbeing of Black women in Britain in ways that are helpful to them, I also recognise that many risks and types of abuse and harm are frequently a part of Black women's digital experiences.

Extending upon this opening chapter, chapter two considers aspects of Black women's media encounters and lives in Britain over the last several decades. Chapter 2 outlines media developments and key matters concerning the on-screen depiction of Black women in Britain. There is discussion of self-representing and organising in relation to Black women and the media, the politics of representation in connection with forms of superficiality, conceptualising Black women's media experiences, representations of Black women on television, and how issues regarding regionality and rurality are embroiled in this. Chapter 2 predominantly draws on archival material and pre-existing written accounts, before Chapter three's stronger emphasis on the contemporary experiences of Black women.

Chapter 3 focuses on Black women's present-day digital, creative, and cultural industry experiences. There is a reflection on the overlap between tacit issues concerning racial, gender, and cultural identity in online spaces, and tensions between the emancipatory, enterprising, enjoyable and extractive dimensions of the digital experiences of Black women in Britain—which are inevitably impacted by capitalist infrastructures and commercial entities.

Chapter 4 highlights issues to do with Black digital diasporic content and communication, as part of discussion of how Black women's digital activity can be a coping mechanism which enables them to deal with experiences of oppression that are specific to their lives and in communal ways. There is a consideration of the resistant credentials of some of the digital experiences of Black women in Britain, while reckoning with potentially conflicting aspects of counter-cultural practices which exist in the context of digital consumerism. This chapter includes analysis of how Black American popular and digital culture contributes to some of the digital encounters and lives of Black women in Britain. There is also a focus on Black women's experiences of natural hair video blogs (vlogs) on YouTube, and knowledge-sharing online.

Chapter 5, which reflects on the impact of the COVID-19 (coronavirus) global pandemic in 2020, includes discussion of the (un)definable nature of the digital experiences of Black women in Britain, and similarities and differences between such experiences. This chapter is a closing consideration of how and why digital terrains continue to be a source of pleasure, creativity, and knowledge-sharing, as well as distress and danger for Black women in Britain.

My writing may have some form of an introduction and conclusion but the story that it is both part and a result of is a complex open-ended one which Black women continue to chronicle—online and offline. Digital (self)representations, discussion, and depiction of the lives of Black women in Britain will continue to far exceed the pages of my book. It is my hope that *The Digital Lives of Black Women in Britain* sheds light on the experiences of such individuals and the structural issues that affect them.

Notes

1. The term 'mixed-race' is commonly used in Britain in reference to a person who is biologically related to parents from different racial backgrounds—broadly defined—including a person with one Black parent of African descent. 'Mixed-race' is one of many terms that has been used as part of essentialising, homogenising, racist, and purist white supremacist pseudoscience discourse regarding race and eugenics. The term 'mixed-race' has also been used as part of some people's self-identifying efforts to distance themselves from their Blackness, in ways that may ultimately be rooted in anti-Black positions and a rejection of Black identity. I use the words 'mixed-race' with caution and an unwaveringly critical perspective of this term, including due to how it can obscure particularities of the experiences of racialised people and can function as part of rhetoric and research which upholds oppressive and racist notions of 'racial purity'. However, I use the words 'mixed-race' in my book to acknowledge how my Black identity—as a child of a Black parent and a white parent—is often perceived, described, and categorised by others in the context of Britain's history and contemporary notions of racial identity and Blackness.
2. 'Black women of African descent' includes Black women with African ancestry who identify as African and those with African ancestry who identify as Caribbean.

References

Adegoke, Yomi. (2019). 'Dark skinned women are now being celebrated, but don't blame us for scepticism.' *Metro*. Last modified 23 August, https://metro.co.uk/2019/08/23/dark-skinned-women-are-now-being-celebrated-but-dont-blame-us-for-scepticism-10619341. Accessed 5 November 2019.

Adewunmi, Bim. (2012). 'Why black British drama is going online, not on TV.' *The Guardian*. Last modified 2 July, https://www.theguardian.com/world/2012/jul/02/black-british-tv-drama-online. Accessed 15 September 2016.

Akiwowo, Seyi. (2018). 'Amnesty's latest research into online abuse finally confirms what Black women have known for over a decade.' *Huffington Post*. Last Modified 19 December, https://www.huffingtonpost.co.uk/entry/amnesty-online-abuse-women-twitter_uk_5c1a0a2fe4b02d2cae8ea0c1. Accessed 17 January 2019.

Akpan, Paula. (2019). 'How the stories of Black women in the UK are being reclaimed.' *Refinery29*. Last modified 10 October, https://www.refinery29.com/en-gb/black-women-history-uk. Accessed 15 October 2019.

Alkalimat, Abdul. (2004). *The African American Experience in Cyberspace: A Resource Guide to the Best Web Sites on Black Culture and History*. London: Pluto Press.

Allman, Esme. (2019). 'The dark side of social media for Black women.' *Black Ballad*. Last Modified 14 February, https://blackballad.co.uk/people/the-dark-side-of-social-media-for-black-women?listIds=5d93b25a88157fff350b6d2e. Accessed 20 February 2019.

Amoah, Susuana. (2019). '#NoShade: A critical analysis of digital influencer activism against shadeism in the beauty industry.' *Academia.edu*. https://www.academia.edu/39881809/NoShade_A_Critical_Analysis_of_Digital_Influencer_Activism_Against_Shadeism_in_the_Beauty_Industry. Accessed 30 July 2019.

Anderson, Monica & Hitlin, Paul. (2016). 'Social media conversations about race: How social media users see, share and discuss race and the rise of hashtags like #BlackLivesMatter.' *Pew Research Center*. Last modified 15 August, http://www.pewinternet.org/2016/08/15/social. Accessed 27 August 2017.

Bailey, Moya. (2010). 'They aren't talking about me ...' *Crunk Feminist Collective*. Last modified 14 March, http://www.crunkfeministcollective.com/2010/03/14/they-arent-talking-about-me/. Accessed 28 March 2020.

Bailey, Moya & Trudy. (2018). 'On misogynoir: citation, erasure, and plagiarism.' *Feminist Media Studies* 18(4): 762–768. https://doi.org/10.1080/14680777.2018.1447395.

Benjamin, Ruha. (2019). *Race After Technology: Abolitionist Tools for the New Jim Code*. Cambridge and Medford, MA: Polity Press.

Berger, John. (2008). *Ways of Seeing* (2nd ed.). London: Penguin.

Bobo, Jacqueline. (ed.) (2001). *Black Feminist Cultural Criticism*. Malden, MA: Blackwell Publishers.
British Social Attitudes. (2013). 'Devolution: trends in national identity.' *Nat Cen Social Research*. https://www.bsa.natcen.ac.uk/latest-report/british-social-attitudes-30/devolution/trends-in-national-identity.aspx. Accessed 15 March 2019.
Brock, André. (2018). 'Critical technocultural discourse analysis.' *New Media & Society* 20(3): 1012–1030. https://doi.org/10.1177/1461444816677532.
Brock, André. (2020). *Distributed Blackness: African American Cybercultures*. New York: New York University Press.
Browne, Simone. (2015). *Dark Matters: On the Surveillance of Blackness*. Durham and London: Duke University Press.
Bruce, Keisha. (Forthcoming, 2022). 'Black women and the curation of digital diasporic intimacy.' PhD Thesis. University of Nottingham.
Bryan, Beverley, Dadzie, Stella & Scafe, Suzanne. (1985). *The Heart of the Race: Black Women's Lives in Britain*. London: Virago.
Bryan, Beverley, Dadzie, Stella & Scafe, Suzanne. (2018). *The Heart of the Race: Black Women's Lives in Britain* (2nd ed.). London: Verso.
Chambers, Eddie. (2017). *Roots & Culture: Cultural Politics in the Making of Black Britain*. London: I.B. Tauris & Co.
Clark, Meredith D. (2014). 'To tweet our own cause: A mixed-methods study of the online phenomenon "Black Twitter".' Chapel Hill, NC: University of North Carolina at Chapel Hill Graduate School, 2014. https://doi.org/10.17615/7bfs-rp55.
Crenshaw, Kimberlé. (1989). 'Demarginalizing the intersection of race and sex: A Black feminist critique of antidiscrimination doctrine, feminist theory and antiracist politics.' *University of Chicago Legal Forum* 1989(1): 139–167. https://chicagounbound.uchicago.edu/uclf/vol1989/iss1/8.
Crenshaw, Kimberlé. (2017). *On Intersectionality: Essential Writings*. New York: The New Press.
Daniels, Jessie. (2009). *Cyber Racism: White Supremacy Online and the New Attack on Civil Rights*. New York: Rowman & Littlefield.
Daniels, Jessie. (2012). 'Race and racism in Internet Studies: A review and critique.' *New Media & Society* 15(5): 695–719. https://doi.org/10.1177/1461444812462849.
Daniels, Jessie. (2017). 'Twitter and white supremacy, a love story.' *DAME Magazine*. Last modified 19 October, https://www.damemagazine.com/2017/10/19/twitter-and-white-supremacy-love-story/. Accessed 10 July 2019.
Daniels, Jessie, Gregory, Karen & McMillan Cottom, Tressie. (eds.) (2017). *Digital Sociologies*. Bristol and Chicago: Policy Press.

Dawes, Laina. (2012). *What Are You Doing Here? A Black Woman's Life and Liberation in Heavy Metal*. Brooklyn. NY: Bazillion Points.

De Kosnik, Abigail & Feldman, Keith P. (eds.) (2019). *#Identity: Hashtagging Race, Gender, Sexuality, and Nation*. Ann Arbor: University of Michigan Press.

Diallo, Rokhaya. (2017). 'When an Afro-feminist festival defies white supremacy.' *Al Jazeera*. Last modified 6 June, https://www.aljazeera.com/indepth/opinion/2017/06/afro-feminist-festival-defies-white-supremacy-170605175645563.html. Accessed 12 November 2018.

Emejulu, Akwugo & McGregor, Callum. (2016). 'Towards a radical digital citizenship in digital education.' *Critical Studies in Education* 60(1): 131–147. https://doi.org/10.1080/17508487.2016.1234494.

Emejulu, Akwugo & Sobande, Francesca. (eds.) (2019). *To Exist is to Resist: Black Feminism in Europe*. London: Pluto Press.

Everett, Anna. (2009). *Digital Diaspora: A Race for Cyberspace*. Albany, NY: SUNY Press.

Figueroa-Vásquez, Yomaira C. (2020). *Decolonizing Diasporas: Radical Mappings of Afro-Atlantic Literature*. Evanston: Northwestern University Press.

Florini, Sarah. (2019). *Beyond Hashtags: Racial Politics and Black Digital Networks*. New York: New York University Press.

Florvil, Tiffany N. & Plumly, Vanessa D. (eds.) (2018). *Rethinking Black German Studies: Approaches, Interventions and Histories*. New York: Peter Lang.

Gabriel, Deborah. (2007). *Layers of Blackness: Colourism in the African Diaspora*. London: Imani Media Ltd.

Gabriel, Deborah. (2016). 'Blogging while Black, British and female: A critical study on discursive activism.' *Information, Communication & Society* 19(11): 1622–1635. https://doi.org/10.1080/1369118X.2016.1146784.

Gilroy, Paul. (1987). *'There Ain't No Black in the Union Jack': The Cultural Politics of Race and Nation*. London: Unwin Hyman.

Gov.uk. (2018). 'Population of England and Wales.' *Gov.uk*. Last modified 1 August, https://www.ethnicity-facts-figures.service.gov.uk/uk-population-by-ethnicity/national-and-regional-populations/population-of-england-and-wales/latest. Accessed 2 March 2019.

Gray, Kishonna L. (2015). 'Race, gender, and virtual inequality: Exploring the liberatory potential of Black cyberfeminist theory.' In *Produsing Theory in a Digital World 2.0: The Intersection of Audiences and Production in Contemporary Theory - Volume 2*, edited by Rebecca Ann Lind, pp. 175–192. New York: Peter Lang.

Gregory, Karen. (2017). 'Structure and agency in a digital world.' In *Digital Sociologies*, edited by Jessie Daniels, Karen Gregory & Tressie McMillan Cottom, pp. 3–7. Bristol and Chicago: Policy Press.

Grier, Sonya A., Thomas, Kevin D. & Johnson, Guillaume D. (2019). 'Reimagining the marketplace: Addressing race in academic marketing research.' *Consumption Markets & Culture*, 22(1): 91–100. https://doi.org/10.1080/10253866.2017.1413800.

Halliday, Aria S. (ed.) (2019). *The Black Girlhood Studies Collection*. Toronto: Women's Press.

hill, layla-roxanne. (2018). 'An Other world.' *Bella Caledonia*. Last modified 8 May, https://bellacaledonia.org.uk/2018/05/08/an-other-world. Accessed 10 May 2018.

hill, layla-roxanne & Sobande, Francesca. (2018). 'In our own words: organising and experiencing exhibitions as Black women and women of colour in Scotland.' In *Accessibility, Inclusion, and Diversity in Critical Event Studies*, edited by Rebecca Finkel, Briony Sharp & Majella Sweeney, pp. 107–121. New York: Routledge.

Hill Collins, Patricia. (2000). *Black Feminist Thought: Knowledge, Consciousness, and the Politics of Empowerment* (2nd ed.). New York and London: Routledge.

Hill Collins, Patricia & Bilge, Sirma. (2016). *Intersectionality*. Cambridge: Polity Press.

Jackson, Sarah. J. (2016). '(Re)imagining intersectional democracy from Black feminism to hashtag activism.' *Women's Studies in Communication* 39(4): 375–379. https://doi.org/10.1080/07491409.2016.1226654.

Johnson, Azeezat. (2019). 'Throwing our bodies against the white background of academia.' *Area* 52(1): 89–96. https://doi.org/10.1111/area.12568.

Johnson, Azeezat, Joseph-Salisbury, Remi & Kamunge, Beth. (eds.) (2018). *The Fire Now: Anti-Racist Scholarship in Times of Explicit Racial Violence*. London: Zed Books.

Johnson, Guillaume D., Thomas, Kevin D., Harrison, Anthony K. & Grier, Sonya A. (eds.) (2019). *Race in the Marketplace: Crossing Critical Boundaries*. Cham: Palgrave Macmillan.

Kay, Jackie. (2010). *Red Dust Road*. London: Picador.

Kolko, Beth E., Nakamura, Lisa & Rodman, Gilbert B. (eds.) (2000). *Race in Cyberspace*. New York and London: Routledge.

Kravets, Olga, Maclaran, Pauline, Miles, Steven & Venkatesh, Alladi. (eds.) (2018). *The SAGE Handbook of Consumer Culture*. London: Sage.

Lewis, Gail. (1993). 'Black women's employment and the British economy.' In *Inside Babylon: The Caribbean Diaspora in Britain*, edited by Winston James & Clive Harris, pp. 73–96. London: Verso.

Lewis, Gail. (2017). Cited in *Black Women Organising*, written by the Brixton Black Women's Group and the Organisation for Women of African and Asian Descent, pp. 1–3. London: Past Tense.

Lewis, Rebecca. (2018). 'Alternative influence: Broadcasting the reactionary right on YouTube.' *Data & Society*. https://datasociety.net/wp-content/uploads/2018/09/DS_Alternative_Influence.pdf. Accessed 15 March 2019.

Lindridge, Andrew, Henderson, Geraldine Rosa & Ekpo, Akon E. (2015). '(Virtual) ethnicity, the Internet, and well-being.' *Marketing Theory* 15(2): 279–285. https://doi.org/10.1177/1470593114553328.

Lu, Jessica H. & Steele, Catherine Knight. (2019). '"Joy is resistance": Cross-platform resilience and (re)invention of Black oral culture online.' *Information, Communication & Society* 22(6): 823–837. https://doi.org/10.1080/1369118X.2019.1575449.

Mbembe, Achille. (2019). 'Notes from the frontier.' *New Humanist* 134(4): 42–46.

McIlwain, Charlton. D. (2020). *Black Software: The Internet and Racial Justice, from the AfroNet to Black Lives Matter*. New York: Oxford University Press.

McMillan Cottom, Tressie. (2017). 'Black cyberfeminism: Ways forward for intersectionality and digital sociology.' In *Digital Sociologies*, edited by Jessie Daniels, Karen Gregory & Tressie McMillan Cottom, pp. 211–231. Bristol and Chicago: Policy Press.

Mercer, Kobena. (1990). 'Black art and the burden of representation.' *Third Text* 4(10): 61–78. https://doi.org/10.1080/09528829008576253.

Mohammed, Wunpini Fatimata. (2019). 'Online activism: Centering marginalized voices in activist work.' *Ada: A Journal of Gender, New Media & Technology* 15. https://adanewmedia.org/2019/02/issue15-mohammed.

Muhammad, Erika Dalya. (2001). 'Race in digital space: Conceptualizing the media project.' *Art Journal* 60(3): 92–95. https://doi.org/10.1080/00043249.2001.10792081.

Mwasi Collectif. (2019). 'Those who fight for us without us are against us: Afro-feminist activism in France'. In *To Exist is to Resist: Black Feminism in Europe*, edited by Akwugo Emejulu & Francesca Sobande, pp. 46–62. London: Pluto Press.

Nakamura, Lisa. (2008). *Digitizing Race: Visual Cultures of the Internet*. Minneapolis: University of Minnesota Press.

Nassy Brown, Jacqueline. (1998). 'Black Liverpool, Black America, and the gendering of diasporic space.' *Cultural Anthropology* 13(3): 291–325. https://doi.org/10.1525/can.1998.13.3.291.

National Records of Scotland. (2018). 'Ethnicity, identity, language and religion.' *Scotland's Census*. Last modified 2018, https://www.scotlandscensus.gov.uk/ethnicity-identity-language-and-religion. Accessed 15 March 2019.

Noble, Safiya Umoja. (2018). *Algorithms of Oppression: How Search Engines Reinforce Racism*. New York: New York University Press.

Noble, Safiya Umoja & Tynes, Brendesha M. (eds.) (2016). *The Intersectional Internet: Race, Sex, Class, and Culture Online*. New York: Peter Lang.

Northern Ireland Statistics and Research Agency. (2013a). 'Census 2011: Detailed characteristics for Northern Ireland on health, religion and national identity [statistics press notice].' *Northern Ireland Statistics and Research Agency*. Last modified 16 May, https://www.nisra.gov.uk/sites/nisra.gov.uk/files/publications/2011-census-results-detailed-characteristics-press-release-16-may-2013.pdf. Accessed 10 March 2019.

Northern Ireland Statistics and Research Agency. (2013b). 'Census 2011— Detailed characteristics for Northern Ireland on ethnicity, country of birth and language [statistics press notice].' *Northern Ireland Statistics and Research Agency*. Last modified 28 June, https://www.nisra.gov.uk/sites/nisra.gov.uk/files/publications/2011-census-results-detailed-characteristics-statistics-bulletin-28-june-2013.pdf. Accessed 10 March 2019.

Nyabola, Nanjala. (2018). *Digital Democracy, Analogue Politics: How the Internet Era is Transforming Politics in Kenya*. London: Zed Books.

Okanlawon, Kafayat. (curator) (2019). *This is Us: Black British Women and Girls*. London: Break the Habit Press.

Omonira-Oyekanmi, Rebecca. (2010). 'The injustice of indefinite detention.' *The Guardian*. Last modified 5 October, https://www.theguardian.com/commentisfree/libertycentral/2010/oct/05/british-immigration-removal-centres-injustice. Accessed 8 October 2019.

Osei, Krys. (2019). 'Fashioning my garden of solace: A Black feminist autoethnography.' *Fashion Theory* 23(6): 733–746. https://doi.org/10.1080/1362704X.2019.1657272.

Otele, Olivette. (2017). 'History of slavery, sites of memory, and identity politics in contemporary Britain.' In *A Stain on Our Past: Slavery and Memory*, edited by Abdoulaye Gueye & Johann Michel, pp. 189–210. Trenton: Africa World Press.

Palma, Annie Yellowe. (2017). *For the Love of a Mother: The Black Children of Ulster*. Gloucester: The Cloister House Press.

Palmer, Lisa Amanda. (2011). 'The politics of loving blackness in the UK.' PhD Thesis. University of Birmingham. https://etheses.bham.ac.uk/id/eprint/1508/. Accessed 7 January 2018.

Palmer, Lisa Amanda. (2016). 'Introduction.' In *Blackness in Britain*, edited by Kehinde Andrews and Lisa Amanda Palmer, pp. 1–6. London: Routledge.

Perlow, Olivia N., Wheeler, Durene I., Bethea, Sharon L. & Scott, Barbara M. (eds.) (2018). *Black Women's Liberatory Pedagogies: Resistance, Transformation, and Healing Within and Beyond the Academy*. Cham: Palgrave Macmillan.

Roberts, Sarah. T. (2019). *Behind the Screen: Content Moderation in the Shadows of Social Media*. New Haven and London: Yale University Press.

Sims, Jennifer Patrice & Njaka, Chinelo L. (2019). *Mixed-Race in the US and UK: Comparing the Past, Present, and Future*. Bingley: Emerald.

Sobande, Francesca. (2017). 'Watching me watching you: Black women in Britain on YouTube.' *European Journal of Cultural Studies* 20(6): 655–671. https://doi.org/10.1177/1367549417733001.

Sobande, Francesca. (2018). 'Managing media as parental race-work: (Re)mediating children's black identities.' In *Consumer Culture Theory: Research in Consumer Behavior* Vol. 19, edited by Samantha N.N. Cross, Cecilia Ruvalcaba, Alladi Venkatesh & Russell W. Belk, pp. 37–53. Bingley: Emerald.

Sobande, Francesca. (2019a). 'Memes, digital remix culture and (re)mediating British politics and public life.' *IPPR Progressive Review* 26(2): 151–160. https://doi.org/10.1111/newe.12155.

Sobande, Francesca. (2019b). 'Woke-washing: 'Intersectional' femvertising and branding 'woke' bravery.' *European Journal of Marketing*, Vol. ahead-of-print No. ahead-of-print. https://doi.org/10.1108/EJM-02-2019-0134.

Sobande, Francesca, Fearfull, Anne & Brownlie, Douglas. (2019). 'Resisting media marginalisation: Black women's digital content and collectivity.' *Consumption Markets & Culture*. https://doi.org/10.1080/10253866.2019.1571491.

Sobande, Francesca & Osei, Krys. (2020). '*An African City*: Black women's creativity, pleasure, diasporic (dis)connections and resistance through aesthetic and media practices and scholarship.' *Communication, Culture & Critique*, tcz024. https://doi.org/10.1093/ccc/tcaa016.

Squires, Catherine, R. (2009). *African Americans and the Media*. Cambridge and Malden, MA: Polity Press.

Steele, Catherine Knight. (2016a). 'The digital barbershop: Blogs and online oral culture within the African American community.' *Social Media + Society* 2(4): 1–10. https://doi.org/10.1177/2056305116683205.

Steele, Catherine Knight. (2016b). 'Signifyin', bitching, and blogging: Black women and resistance discourse online.' In *The Intersectional Internet: Race, Sex, Class, and Culture Online*, edited by Safiya Umoja Noble & Brendesha M. Tynes, pp. 73–93. New York: Peter Lang.

Steele, Catherine Knight. (2017). 'Black bloggers and their varied publics: The everyday politics of black discourse online.' *Television & New Media* 19(2): 112–127. https://doi.org/10.1177/1527476417709535.

Sulter, Maud. (1986). 'Surveying the scene: Writings by women of African and Asian descent.' In March 1986 Issue (27) of the *Greater London Council Women's Committee Bulletin*, pp. 28–29.

Tate, Shirley Anne. (2009). *Black Beauty: Aesthetics, Stylization, Politics*. Farnham: Ashgate Publishing.

Tate, Shirley Anne. (2017a). *The Governmentality of Black Beauty Shame: Discourse, Iconicity and Resistance*. Basingstoke: Palgrave Macmillan.

Tate, Shirley Anne. (2017b). 'Skin: Post-feminist bleaching culture and the political vulnerability of blackness.' In *Aesthetic Labour: Rethinking Beauty Politics in Neoliberalism*, edited by Ana Sofia Elias, Rosalind Gill & Christina Scharff, pp. 199–213. Basingstoke: Palgrave Macmillan.

Taylor, Keeanga-Yamahtta. (2016). *From #BlackLivesMatter to Black Liberation*. Chicago: Haymarket Books.

The Afro-Caribbean Women's Association. (1990). 'Our day of awakening.' In *Grit and Diamonds: Women in Scotland Making History 1980–1990*, edited by In Shirley Henderson & Alison Mackay, pp. 121–122. Edinburgh: Stramullion Ltd and The Cauldron Collective.

The Brixton Black Women's Group and the Organisation for Women of African and Asian Descent. (2017). *Black Women Organising*. London: Past Tense.

Twine, France Winddance. (2004). 'A white side of black Britain: The concept of racial literacy.' *Ethnic and Racial Studies* 27(6): 878–907. https://www.tandfonline.com/doi/abs/10.1080/0141987042000268512.

Twine, France Winddance. (2010). *A White Side of Black Britain: Interracial Intimacy and Racial Literacy*. Durham and London: Duke University Press.

Walcott, Rianna. (Forthcoming, 2021). 'A tweet at the table: Black British women's identity expression on social media.' PhD Thesis. King's College, London.

Wekker, Gloria. (2016). *White Innocence: Paradoxes of Colonialism and Race*. Durham and London: Duke University Press.

Wherry, Frederick F. (2012). *The Culture of Markets*. Malden, MA and Cambridge: Polity Press.

Williams, Raymond. (2003). *Television: Technology and Cultural Form* (3rd ed.). London: Routledge.

Wilson-Ojo, Madeline. (2017). 'Social media has done for Black British women in one decade what TV couldn't in thirty years.' *The Huffington Post*. Last modified 17 December, https://www.huffingtonpost.co.uk/entry/black-women-social-media_uk_5a36b3d2e4b0e7f1200cfc1b. Accessed 20 December 2017.

Yancy, George. (2018). *Backlash: What Happens When We Talk Honestly about Racism in America*. Lanham, MD: Rowman & Littlefield.

Young, Lola. (2000). 'What is Black British feminism?' *Women: A Cultural Review* 11(1–2) 45–60. https://doi.org/10.1080/09574040050051415.

CHAPTER 2

Black Women and the Media in Britain

Abstract This chapter outlines media developments and key matters concerning the on-screen depiction of Black women in Britain in recent decades. It draws on material accessed at the Black Cultural Archives (BCA) in Brixton, London and the Spare Rib digital archive at the British Library. This chapter discusses self-representing and organising in relation to Black women and the media. The discussion explores the politics of representation in connection with superficiality, conceptualisations of Black women's media experiences and television representations, as well as the influence of variations regarding regionality and rurality. This chapter emphasises that due to the geo-culturally and socio-politically specific setting of Britain—and its consititutive nations—work focused on the lives of Black women (t)here demands a critical lens that is sensitive to this context's various characteristics.

Keywords Activism · Black archives · Black women · Britain · Representation · Television

> Here are Black women writing, unapologetically and with no holds barred, to, about, and for other Black women, using our own words, in a way that has not often been attempted before. (Melba Wilson 1982, p. 31)

© The Author(s) 2020
F. Sobande, *The Digital Lives of Black Women in Britain*,
Palgrave Studies in (Re)Presenting Gender,
https://doi.org/10.1007/978-3-030-46679-4_2

Published by the European Parliament in 1995, a European Women's Lobby report on the experiences of Black and migrant women in Europe noted the persistence of racism and far-right politics across the continent—paired with the ambivalence of governments that bore witness to this injustice. More than two decades later, little has changed. Black women in Europe continue to face insidious institutional anti-Black racism and interrelated oppression that can severely impact their health (Cole 2018; Emejulu and Sobande 2019; Walcott 2020). Today, Black women in Britain deal with the force of Euroscepticism that is often steeped in nationalistic and racist concepts of citizenship and Britishness, as well as the effects of backlash against neoliberal notions of multiculturalism, which the scholarship of political sociologist Akwugo Emejulu (2016) addresses. In sum, 'our right to be here is questioned almost daily by politicians and the media' (Bryan et al. 2018, p. 3).

Since its European Union (EU) referendum outcome in 2016, Britain's planned and eventual exit (Brexit) from the EU on 31 January 2020, has been linked to increasing racist hate crimes (Benson and Lewis 2019). Although such a political climate undoubtedly impacts Black women in Britain, it is crucial to acknowledge that these same women have experienced and documented discrimination at the nexus of anti-Black racism, sexism, classism, xenophobia, and other interlocking relations of power, long before Brexit (Bassel and Emejulu 2017; Bryan et al. 1985; Lewis 1993; Ngcobo 1987; Palmer 2011; Sulter 1985; the Brixton Black Women's Group and the Organisation for Women of African and Asian Descent 2017; Young 2000).

It is important to comprehend the intersecting nature of oppressions as 'social inequality is rarely caused by a single factor' (Hill Collins and Bilge 2016, p. 26). Efforts to understand the contemporary lives of Black women in Britain, including their digital encounters, require recognition of experiences of intersecting oppressions, as well as political organising and active production and critique of media and cultural spheres in past decades. Considering connected issues involves unpacking key concepts, theories, and perspectives that have played a central role in Black women's scholarly, literary, creative, grassroots, and everyday meditations on their lives and media experiences—then and now.

In turn, I draw on tenets of Black feminism which can be understood as being 'both a theory and a politics of affirmation and liberation' (Emejulu and Sobande 2019, p. 3)—based on the lives of Black women of African descent. I am also spurred on by the impetus of the anti-racist scholarship of Azeezat Johnson et al. (2018) which is 'about taking stock and bearing witness to the racial conditions in which we find ourselves' (p. 2). Before chapter three's stronger focus on the contemporary experiences of Black women in Britain, this chapter draws particularly on archival material and pre-existing written accounts. Discussion in the following sections of this chapter acknowledges that due to the geo-culturally and socio-politically specific context of Britain and its constitutive nations, work focused on the lives of Black women (t)here demands a critical lens that is sensitive to the characteristics of this setting (Bryan et al. 1985; Linton and Walcott 2018; Media Diversified 2016; Nassy Brown 1998; Obasi 2019; Omonira-Oyekanmi 2010; Palmer 2011; Perry 2016; Sims and Njaka 2019; Twine 2004, 2010).

SELF-REPRESENTING AND ORGANISING AROUND BLACK WOMEN AND THE MEDIA

As a rare national heritage centre which is committed to archiving and celebrating African and Caribbean histories, the Black Cultural Archives (BCA) in Brixton, is an invaluable source of information concerning decades of Black life in Britain. BCA is a space which contains writing, images and materials that symbolise how Black people have strived to record their histories, while speaking for and representing themselves in a context—Britain—located within an unshakeable ongoing colonial legacy (Gilroy 1987; Lewis 1993, 2000; Otele 2017, 2019; Owusu 2018; Perry 2016).

It is important to recognise that archives exist in many forms, including non-tangible and living ones (Hall 2001; Larasi 2019). Although for now, BCA is the only national heritage centre in Britain dedicated to archiving the history and contemporary experiences of Black people (t)here, myriad personal, digital, collectively gathered, lived, and privately kept Black archives exist in Britain. Therefore, whenever accessing material at BCA, I do so with an awareness of how absences in an archive do not equate to the non-existence of experiences, ephemera, documents, materials, thoughts, creative works, images, conversations, stories, and memories that are not present in that specific space (Sharpe 2016).

I write this only days after recent news regarding the financial difficulties that BCA faces. It is a centre that the government presently—in

October 2018—does not fund, and in any case government funding could constrain the agency and politics of Black people involved in its direction. The collective, creative, and cultural pursuits of Black people in Britain—particularly Black women from working-class backgrounds—have often lacked substantial funding and institutional backing. In addition, due to pervasive 'neoliberal brand culture' (Banet-Weiser 2018, p. 13), such work is always at risk of being compromised and co-opted, including as a result of structurally white institutions becoming financially involved. Hence, decades of self-publication, self-representation, and community organising among Black women in Britain, which is now shaped by 'online content creation that enables the expression of political and social issues in dialogic and powerful ways, challenging the dominance of discussions led by traditional news outlets and gatekeepers' (Sobande 2019a, p. 152).

The vital scholarship and work of Black women such as historian Jade Bentil (forthcoming, 2021) provide insightful writing and research regarding Black women's experiences and resistance in Britain, especially during the late 1940s to late 1980s (Akpan 2019). The crucial collective-building activities of Black women in Britain include the formation of the Brixton Black Women's Group (BBWG) in 1973 (Lewis and Hemmings 2019) which campaigned and challenged structural inequalities concerning the lives of Black women, ranging from reproductive rights and labour experiences, to the provision of healthcare and education. The slightly later founding of the Organisation of Women of African and Asian Descent (OWAAD) in 1978 also reflects how Black women in Britain have worked to tackle systemic interconnected oppression and strive for societal change. In the words of Melba Wilson (1982), who has worked extensively across the areas of public policy, health, and social welfare, 'Black women themselves are the ones who should and will make the rules and set the standards against which they are to be judged' (p. 31).

As media and cultural industries scholars such as David Hesmondhalgh and Anamik Saha (2013) outline, '[c]ultural production in the modern world cannot be adequately understood without taking account of race and ethnicity, and their relation to oppression' (p. 180). In agreement with this perspective, and extending upon such a statement, I affirm the need for related research to investigate how issues regarding race and ethnicity—more specifically, anti-Blackness—intersect with those concerning gender, class, dis/ability, homophobia, xenophobia, transphobia, and other interdependent forms of systemic oppression.

The nuanced experiences of Black people in Britain are often overlooked and/or reduced to (re)presentations emptied of substance as part of dominant discourse pertaining to media, the creative and cultural industries, inequality, and public life. Nevertheless, some of the experiences of Black people in Britain have been the focus of critical events and dialogue over the decades, including the following: a November 1988 conference report on Black People, Human Rights and The Media (Black Rights [UK] 1988), The Race and New Technology Conference 1985 (Morris 1986), Association of Black Film and Video workshops in the 1980s, as well as an International Women's Week event in 1986 at The Black-Art Gallery in London, titled 'And all of us are strong': Discussing Black Women's Art.

The Black Women and Media Conference (14–15 April) at The Factory in West London in 1984, which was attended by over 150 women, 'provided space for Black women and women of colour to talk about different aspects of the media in this country as well as a chance to share their skills' (Spare Rib 1984a, p. 18). Such an event exemplifies how for decades Black women have actively addressed issues concerning intersecting inequalities and the media in Britain. Second-wave feminist magazine, Spare Rib (1984a), describes the Black Women and Media Conference as having involved workshops to discuss topics such as (p. 18):

> Black women's access to the media, the media's role in perpetuating racism and sexism, a Black women's media network, access to the media and sharing skills, training courses and control of images presented of Black women in the media, and how the feminist media/Black media could be made more accountable to Black women's needs and issues.

A workshop on 'Black Women and the Media' at the second National Black Women's Conference coordinated by OWAAD (29–30 March) in Tottenham, North London, in 1980, further indicates how Black women in Britain have been collectively organising around issues connected to their media experiences for many years.

More recently, co-founded by Paula Akpan and Nicole Crentsil in 2017, Black Girl Festival is a vibrant annual event that takes place in London and brings together Black women, girls and, non-binary people as part of a day of workshops, panel discussions and activities that focus on issues that are particular to their lives—including, but not limited to, matters to do with the arts, media, publishing, and the creative and cultural industries. In previous decades, conferences specifically focused on Black women's experiences and Black feminism in Britain included a two-day event from 19–20 May at University of London Union in 1984 (Spare Rib 1984b), attended by Black women from parts of Britain such as Bristol, Edinburgh, and Leicester. Writing about such events in the 1980s acknowledges specific isolation felt by Black women outside of London (Spare Rib 1984b) which serves as a reminder of the role of regionality in experiences of Black life in Britain, especially in parts where distinctly few Black people live.

In addition, as writer Marla Bishop (1987) wrote about in Spare Rib, Black women in Britain have engaged with the creative work of Black women in the US 'to redress the balance of the visibility of Black women on film' (p. 32). Such efforts in the 1980s included supporting the screening of a package of films by directors Ayoka Chenzira and Julie Dash which were shown at regional British cinemas including Chapter, Cardiff (April 2) and Filmhouse, Edinburgh (April 15–16). As is discussed in more detail in chapter four, when interviewing Black women in Britain about their media experiences, many who I spoke to enacted, what may be described as 'discursive forays into "black America"' (Nassy Brown 1998, p. 291)—commenting on how depictions of, and, discussions led by Black women in the US shaped their own media experiences and lives.

In the present-day context of Scotland, the work of individuals including writer, curator, artist, and organiser layla-roxanne hill who advocates for non-commodifiable collective liberation, foregrounds the creative and lived experiences of Black women who are most structurally oppressed due to the workings of anti-Black racism, sexism, classism, homophobia and xenophobia. hill's work includes many years of grass-roots and collective activism, in addition to her co-organisation of events and activities in collaboration with the National Union of Journalists Scotland, and The Race Beat—a UK media network for people of colour (hill 2017, 2019). There is no shortage of examples of consciousness-raising and collaboration between Black women in Britain (Bryan et al. 2018). However, there is limited scholarship regarding the role of digital media in this, and, to draw on the Black feminist words of writer and activist Audre Lorde (1988), as part of 'how we deal with each other across our own differences as Black women' (p. 39).

Although 'the mid-1950s is taken as the point when Black people began to settle in Britain in significant numbers' (Ngcobo 1987, p. viii), such a presence in Britain long predates the twentieth-century, including due to the impact of colonialism and the enslavement of Black people. After Windrush—which involved the mass migration of Black Caribbean people to Britain between the late 1940s and the start of the 1970s (Brinkhurst-Cuff 2018), the 1980s yielded a somewhat changing landscape of Black women's representation in Britain. Such changes included Labour party politician Diane Abbott becoming the first Black woman to be elected to the House of Commons in 1987 and who has continued to serve as a Member of Parliament (MP) for Hackney North and Stoke Newington since then.

Titled 'Black and Ethnic Minority Women', the March 1986 Issue (27) of the Greater London Council Women's Committee Bulletin provides a vivid snapshot of life for some Black women in Britain then. The Issue opens by highlighting that it is likely to be the last of the Bulletin's three-year span (1983–1986), which commenced with an inaugural issue in celebration of what is referred to as the 'Anti-Racist Year'. The Bulletin was produced at a time when notions of solidarity between people from perceived 'minority ethnic groups', based on a shared anti-racist, anti-capitalist, and anti-imperialist political position—since then dubbed 'political blackness'—meant that the term 'Black' was not exclusively used in relation to Black people of African descent. Instead, 'Black' was also sometimes used in reference to those of Asian descent and other individuals identified as 'ethnic minorities' (Maylor 2009)—in ways that can diminish and deny distinct differences between people, including experiences and perpetuation of oppression (Jameela, forthcoming, 2020). As the Cruel Ironies Collective (2019, p. 187) state in reference to political blackness:

> When Black people and non-Black people are homogenised into a single category based on sameness this can potentially serve to hide and/or deny anti-Blackness. The fantasy in which non-Black people of colour are unable to oppress Black people is upheld by ignoring the lived experience of Black people who have structurally experienced anti-Blackness from non-Black people of colour.

Formations of '[s]olidarity between different racialised women can never be taken for granted' (Emejulu and Sobande 2019, p. 6). Furthermore, as educator and writer Lola Okolosie accounts for in the forward of the republished version of *The Heart of the Race: Black Women's Lives in Britain* (Bryan et al. 2018), 'Thirty years on from its initial reception, 'black' as a political identity under which empire's unaccounted-for-children could unite has become hotly contested' (Okolosie 2018, p. xi), and rightly so. Thus, when reading the March 1986 Issue (27) of the Greater London Council Women's Committee Bulletin, I did so with an awareness of the racial politics in Britain at that time—the 1980s—and the need to carefully identify how the term 'Black' was used in all of the literature I came across and in reference to whom.

The March 1986 Issue (27) of the Bulletin documents the existence of the London New Technology Network's Women's Training Course Project Group, which was linked to work that addressed the information communication technology (ICT) experiences of 'Black and minority ethnic (BME)[1] women'—such as via the Minorities Information Technology Awareness Group (MITAG). As is evident when reading the Bulletin, power relations embedded in ICT, and critiques of how they impact different people, have been around for a long time before the rise of online content-sharing platforms and social media such as Twitter, Instagram, Facebook and YouTube. This is notable when reflecting on the creation of groups decades ago, such as The MITAG Women's Unit which was based in Camden and involved efforts to challenge the patriarchal and paternalistic way that ICT training was often delivered (Morris 1986).

In the 1980s there was already anxiety about the possibility that ICT could prove to be detrimental to the health and wellbeing of racialised people through an increasing sense of alienation. Shaped by what may be referred to as 'victim/agent dualisms' (Kanai 2019, p. 16), such concerns included the worry that women would be isolated due to the potential for new technology to make them 'passive objects with no control over the technology' (Morris 1986, p. 40). In Britain today there are similar worries, and, sometimes, indications of unwarranted moral panic surrounding the potential for digital technology to lead to social isolation. There are also continued assumptions that even once people have sustained access to and understandings of new technology, individuals from structurally oppressed social demographics—including Black people—are intrinsically incapable of using this technology in active and agentic ways. Such assumptions are often buttressed by systemically discriminatory perceptions of people's (in)abilities, which in some cases are based on classist, anti-Black, and xenophobic points of view, alongside the normativity of how whiteness is associated with technology, digital literacy, and so-called 'progress' and 'advancement' (Hobson 2008).

Still, concerns articulated in the March 1986 Issue (27) of the Greater London Council Women's Committee Bulletin—penned when the 'computer age' (Spare Rib 1992, p. 58) was perceived as 'taking its toll' (ibid.) on people's health and wellbeing—are not misguided. Views also recorded in Spare Rib (1992) illustrate a point in history when many worries about the potentially hazardous impact of ICT on women's health predominantly focused on physical dimensions of this, such as headaches and effects on posture and reproductive biology. However, such perspectives were formed before the rise of online harassment and abuse which can impact both physical and mental health, and such points of view also predated the more widespread realisation of the agency that women can now exert online—albeit, in ways that are structurally restrictive.

Accordingly, chapter three features a discussion of how the contemporary digital experiences of Black women in Britain can benefit them in various ways, and, for some, involve 'do-it-together' (DIT) content creation and a sense of collectiveness which is a far cry from social alienation. There is also reflection on some of the many dangers that Black women in Britain deal with online. Before considering such issues, I reckon with the messy and ubiquitous politics of representation in society, while affirming that although representations are often far from being radical, revolutionary, or resistant in nature, representations and the processes that result in their production are always political.

THE POLITICS OF REPRESENTATION

The expression 'representation matters' often prompts mixed responses and many questions concerning how representation is being defined, whose representation is being referred to, and, as has been extensively studied by sociologists, cultural theorists and political activists such as Stuart Hall, what the function of such representation is (Hall 1997; Hall et al. 2012). The media and communications scholarship of Sarah Banet-Weiser (2018) explicates the persistence of a contemporary 'economy of visibility' (p. 2), within which representations—including those associated with popular feminism—are valued for their ability to increase the visibility of something or someone, as opposed to their capacity to contribute to substantial sustained action and social change. Attuned to digital culture and constant demand for attention and viral content online, Banet-Weiser's (2018) conceptualisation of an 'economy of visibility' (p. 2) captures 'a media landscape that is many things at once: a technological and economic context devoted to the accumulation of views, clicks, "likes", etcetera' (ibid.).

Banet-Weiser's (2018) insightful examination of the relationship between consumer culture, capital, media representations, marketing, popular feminism, and visibility elucidates the spectacle surrounding depictions of people and social movements in commercial campaigns and content. Returning to such work on an 'economy of visibility' (Banet-Weiser 2018, p. 2), in chapter three I consider how (re)presentations of Black people feature as part of the digital marketing content of creative and cultural industry organisations in Britain—objectifying and spectacularising Black people in ways that suit institutions' self-serving communications strategies.

In some cases, representations that appear in media and marketplace settings are inextricably linked to what sociologist Herman Gray (2004) refers to as being 'the Struggle for "Blackness"', 'Black Cultural Politics and Commercial Culture' (Gray 2004, p. 1), as well as elements of viral and clickbait digital culture (Gray 2015). Gray's (2004) scholarship on race, television and Blackness includes observation that amid 'the contemporary politics of black popular culture, much critical attention has been given to identity and expressive culture' (p. 1), and such 'critical discourses and the popular attention they have generated play a strategic role in the maintenance of and challenge to various systems of domination' (ibid.).

The work of Africana studies scholar Marquita Marie Gammage (2016) also provides sharp analysis of issues regarding Black media depictions, by examining media portrayals of Black women and how they communicate ideas about Blackness to a watchful public. Furthermore, focusing on the context of Britain, the work of marketing communications scholar Deborah Gabriel (2016) illustrates how Black women have represented themselves in the blogosphere in ways that have enabled 'discursive activism to challenge stereotypical raced and gendered representation in the mainstream media' (p. 1622).

Media and political representation can play a useful part in collective, activist, resistant, and social justice-oriented work. More specifically, as I outline as part of prior analysis of 'memes, digital remix culture and (re)mediating British politics and public life' (Sobande 2019a, p. 153):

Associated with a 'do it yourself' (DIY) or 'do it together' (DIT) ethos, digital remix culture involves the (re)production of various forms of media by people on the internet, including individuals without formal media training. Often by blending pop culture and political references, remixed digital content results in commentary that reflects different public conversations, contestations and concerns about the current state of politics and society.

Digital remix culture, including the widespread and strategic use of memes and GIFs, can arguably contribute to meaningful media, political critiques, and, perhaps, interventions, such as through 'the repurposing of photographs and the words of politicians and public figures, yielding acerbic statements that can be as critical and/or offensive as they are humorous' (Sobande 2019a, p. 153). However, the potential toxicity and superficiality of examples of media representation, both in digital spaces and elsewhere, include how entangled aspects of a represented person's identity (e.g. their race, gender, sexuality, and class) are assumed to be tethered to certain political perspectives—including, in some cases, so-called 'progressive' ones that are attributed to a wider social group that they are deemed to be part of.

As is explained in sociologist and African American studies scholar Ruha Benjamin's (2019) leading work on *Race After Technology*, '[e]conomic recognition is a ready but inadequate proxy for political representation and social power' (p. 19). Contrary to what is sometimes alluded to by the expression 'representation matters', an increase in the media representation of people from a systemically oppressed social demographic does not equate to, or, reflect, structural moves towards a more equitable society (Warner 2017). 'Representation matters' may be uttered as part of reductive claims that the mere presence of more Black women in media and political domains advances Black women's alleged inherent and shared political position—an assumed unified politics that is implied to equally prioritise *all* Black women's lives and struggles.

This is further illustrated by the necessary and in-depth research of social geographer Azeezat Johnson (2017) whose work affirms the importance of acknowledging and understanding nuanced differences between forms of structural oppression experienced by Black women. Johnson (2017) examines how the persistent entanglements of anti-Black racism, sexism, and Islamophobia specifically impact Black Muslim women in Britain. These observations of Johnson's (2017) are evident in the comments of Poppy—one of 26 Black women[2] who I interviewed as part of research that informed this book.

Poppy is a Black Muslim woman and mother of young children who referred to herself as being between '37 and 40 years old'. She is based in Scotland where she has lived since moving there years ago from a city in West Africa. When I met with Poppy, she spoke in detail about her decision to turn down an opportunity to appear in a media project in Scotland about Black life there, despite her strong personal and professional interest in such issues:

> I wasn't quite comfortable with the idea of featuring in a media project because of my accent, and thought my accent might put people off...I thought, they [Black people] are the silent minority, nobody knows them, why don't we celebrate them. I didn't know if I'd be accepted and I wear the hijab and I just thought...are they ready for a Muslim woman on the screen? She's Black, she's [laughs] she's got an accent, she's got a hijab on, she's this and that...

Poppy was the only woman I interviewed who explicitly discussed how the entanglements of anti-Blackness, sexism, misogyny, xenophobia, and Islamophobia impact Black Muslim women in Britain, and, as in Poppy's case, can deter and prevent some such women from pursuing media industry aspirations. Poppy's comments implicitly point to the futility of media industry 'diversity' initiatives which are marketed as enabling Black peoples' entry into careers in the industry, but which fail to identify institutional measures to support such individuals in the likely event that their hyper-visibility in the media leads to abuse from the public—including anti-Black, xenophobic, sexist, misogynistic, and Islamophobic abuse, which is also impacted by colourism.

Experiences of venomous anti-Black racism and Islamophobia that Poppy spoke to me about are a snapshot of numerous examples of how, contrary to the message of much public discourse, Scotland is far from being a so-called 'post-racial' society that is tolerant of all people (Folorunso 2019). Of the 14 Black women in Scotland who I interviewed, all spoke about anti-Black racism in that context—from their own painful experiences to those of their children, friends, and family. Poppy discussed how markers of her racial, religious, gender, and ethnic identity are interpreted in discriminatory ways that result in her being positioned as a hyper-visible Black African Muslim woman who is socially located outside of narrow notions of Scottish [white] identity.

Poppy acknowledged that Scotland has a creative industries landscape (Wells and Valencia 2017) but spoke about there being less media industry opportunities for Black women in Scotland than those that appear to be available in England—where there are more cities identified as creative and cultural hubs (Allen and Hollingworth 2013) and with larger populations of Black people. This observation should not be mistaken for suggesting that there is anywhere in Britain where Black women do not experience structural oppression and challenges in terms of their pursuit of media, creative, and cultural industry opportunities—far from it. Instead, Poppy's observation, which was echoed by the other Black women in Scotland who I spoke to, reflects how such challenges may be exacerbated by regional factors which link to the (un)availability of industry opportunities and the extent to which different Black women are (in)visible and hyper-visible.

When reflecting on the salient nature of her identity as a Black African Muslim woman in Scotland, and how she subsequently navigates media opportunities, Poppy alluded to forms of strategic (in)visibility and intentional opacity (Glissant 1997) which can play a part in how some Black women in Britain negotiate tensions between desire and demand for their representation, and the prospect of subsequent surveillance, harassment, abuse and danger that their visibility may prompt. The relevant concept of 'aesthetic-political space' (Scott cited in Scott et al. 2016, p. 5) encompasses how the aesthetic and ideological are intrinsically linked in ways resulting in visual expressions of political and personal meanings, including in the form of media imagery. As 'visual media are ever more the vehicle by which people make sense of their racialized and gendered world' (Joseph 2019, p. 27), learning about people's experiences of such media can aid understanding of co-constitutive issues concerning identity, inequality, and ideology.

Although magazines such as British Vogue, now under the direction of Edward Enninful, have started to feature more Black women on their pages and covers, in 2017 there were months when none of Britain's best-selling magazine covers featured a Black person (Hirsch 2018). The limited depiction of Black women in Britain in the media, as well as their treatment within the industry, continues to be a source of frustration for some (Olumide 2019). This is expressed in online articles including 'News Blackout – Why Aren't Black British Women Treated Fairly In the Media?' (hill 2017), 'Who Stole All the Black Women from Britain?' (Dabiri 2013), and 'Why black British drama is going online, not on TV' (Adewunmi 2012).

Those I interviewed spoke of their efforts to avoid specific media outlets which they identified as often communicating stereotypical ideas and images of Black women, which promote anti-Black and sexist ideologies that are connected to a 'white imaginary' and 'white mainstream media' bolstered by heteronormative and patriarchal positions. Such perspectives connect to the inimitable words of writer, editor, scholar, and so much more—Toni Morrison (2017, p. 37):

> Far from our original expectations of increased intimacy and broader knowledge, routine media presentations deploy images and language that narrow our view of what humans look like (or ought to look like) and what in fact we are like.

As is unpacked in the following chapters, for some Black women in Britain, their rejection of various mainstream media channels forms part of wider and strategic attempts to create and source media depictions of, by, and benefitting, Black women—outside of the claustrophobic confines of mainstream mass-media in Britain (Sobande 2017; Sobande et al. 2019).

From tourism activity that is dependent on 'the association of blackness with servitude' (Wilkes 2016, p. 8), to brands that attempt to perform a proximity to Blackness (Crockett 2008), there is an extensive list of examples of how ideas about Blackness, images of Black people, and Black people themselves, are used as part of consumer culture (Sobande 2019b). At times, representations are nothing more than shallow, surface-level, and tokenistic in their makeup—devoid of any connection to substantial social change or political commitments and liberationist goals. Even so, from literary settings to the small screens of mobile devices, representations of Black women continue to be constructed, deconstructed, and reconstructed by them in meaningful ways that are worthy of acknowledging and understanding (Bobo 1995, 2001; Gabriel 2016; Melancon 2014).

Departing from the ambiguous, easily contorted, and, sometimes meaningless, notion that 'representation matters', my book is more firmly grounded in the belief that representation is political, regardless of any attempts to profess its neutrality and objectivity. Moreover, despite the frequent focus on media depictions and the image of people in public-facing roles, I affirm that discussion and writing about the politics of representation must equally attend to who is present in media production activities, why they are, how they are treated, as well as how such concerns connect with material conditions and ideological infrastructures (Warner 2017).

Conceptualising Black Women's Media Representation and Experiences

Media depictions present people with 'the reimagined, reinvented version of the real' (hooks 2009, p. 1), and media's weighty influence in society includes its capacity to transmit political positions and reflect structural power relations. Media images and the meaning-making that they catalyse can appear to be a unifying communication force, while also mirroring social hierarchies. As has been raised by Black women and Black feminist writers, activists, creatives, cultural commentators, critics, and scholars, Black women have been (mis)represented and maligned in media, visual culture, and public life throughout history (Bryan et al. 2018). Their image and labour has also frequently been exploited in the service of capitalism and its patriarchal, racist, sexist, heteronormative, colonialist, and ableist underpinnings (Davis 1981).

Conversely, Black women around the world produce and share media content as part of resistant and activist work which challenges the structural conditions that diminish their quality of life, as well as the lives of others. Among examples of this is the use of hashtags (Jackson et al. 2017, 2020) and social media to raise awareness of the police brutality, violence, and oppression that is aimed at Black women (Omonira-Oyekanmi 2016)—including interlocking transphobia, cis-sexism, misogyny and anti-Black racism that Black trans* women face; all of which is commonly under-reported and misrepresented in mainstream mass-media in Britain (Alabanza 2018; Brinkhurst-Cuff 2019).

Media and marketplace environments are filled with symbols and scenarios spawned by racism and colonialism (Grier et al. 2019; Johnson et al. 2019; Sobande 2019b) which can contribute to people's perceptions of others, as well as their self-perceptions. Media depictions and the narratives that they are couched in can distinctly impact the lives of Black women, even as children 'who are often told from an early age that we have to be more aware of how others perceive us, how we appear in society is often more important than asserting our individuality' (Dawes 2012, p. 49). The groundbreaking work of information and communication studies scholar Safiya Umoja Noble (2018) highlights the oppressiveness of algorithms and the racist content yielded by online search engines. Such scholarship emphasises that, from childhood, Black women are often societally spectacularised and framed as hypersexualised, due to interlocking anti-Black racism, sexism, misogyny and other interconnected power dynamics (Noble 2018).

The work of both Noble and educational psychology and African American studies scholar Brendesha M. Tynes (2016) outlines how intersecting oppressions occur online and in relation to representations of Black women (Noble 2018). Relatedly, the preeminent Black feminist scholarship of sociologist Patricia Hill Collins (2000), which explicates a societal matrix of domination, is crucial to understanding how Black women are portrayed as part of 'controlling images' that are 'externally defined'. Hill Collins (2000) explains how instrumentalised stereotypes and associated images of Black women, created by other people, have been used for centuries as part of a matrix of dominant oppressive ideological efforts that contribute to their structural mistreatment.

The scholarship of Hill Collins (2000) stresses that controlling images of Black women contrast with those of white womanhood which are promulgated through 'the cult of true womanhood' (p. 72); positioning white women as racially unmarked women and Black women as being 'the Other'. Many controlling stereotypes have doggedly followed the depiction of Black women in media (Bailey 2020), including those that frame them as stoic, predatory, fetishised, and exoticised. Efforts to break stereotypes may be rooted in an aim to tackle oppressive structures and power relations, but as is outlined in the writing of cultural producer Tobi Kyeremateng (2019), obsessions with breaking stereotypes can involve pandering to 'the lens of whiteness'.

In 1992, Black feminist, scholar, and activist bell hooks asserted that there was a relative scarcity of writing by Black women which specifically focuses on their gaze and encounters as spectators. In addition to hooks' many years of work that foregrounds such issues in the US, Black feminist and women's studies scholar Jacqueline Bobo (2001) has vividly written about related matters—including Black women's creative, media, and cultural contributions, and formation of interpretive communities. Bobo (2001) writes about how Black women take part in the 'work of reclamation and redefinition' (p. 5) via their participation in and creation of media and cultural contexts, as active creators and spectators rather than mere passive consumers. Since the publication of *Black Looks: Race and*

Representation by hooks (1992), *Black Feminist Cultural Criticism* by Bobo (2001), and *Black Feminist Thought: Knowledge, Consciousness, and the Politics of Empowerment* by Hill Collins (2000), scholarship by Black women and about their media and cultural experiences has expanded.

Regardless, in the context of media and cultural studies, and associated fields of research in Britain, such work remains relatively scant. Often when Black women's perspectives *have* appeared in such scholarly output, they have done so via the words of non-Black researchers, including those who do not tarry with how their own positionality and politics is implicated in their work and (mis)readings of Black women's lives. Some research in the field may be deemed part of what Nadine Chambers (2019) insightfully identifies as being 'the difficulty of how anti-Blackness can arrive disguised as social justice work and/or academic scholarship' (p. 31)—discussed in detail in Chambers' independent research on Black and Indigenous geographies.

Also, as is affirmed by sociologists Jennifer Patrice Sims and Chinelo L. Njaka (2019, p. 2), '[t]he different linguist manners and rhetorical strategies used to ask about race within the US and UK, despite both having a dominant colourblind ideology, underscores how race is differentially constructed in the two nations'. Such explanations emphasise the need for work about the lives of Black women in Britain which considers the complexities of this specific context and the current political climate, alongside longstanding anti-Black structures that they are traversing. The following paragraphs discuss the experiences of Black women among different generations, including those that are part of a Black diaspora that 'came of age in a context of world-transforming dislocations at national, regional, and global levels' (Scott cited in Scott et al. 2016, p. 4).

REPRESENTATIONS OF BLACK WOMEN ON TELEVISION

The media landscape in Britain includes well established and mainstream television, print, radio and film outlets, as well as independent start-up production companies, digital-only media spaces and content created by people online. Although social media turned out to be the focus of a lot of my discussions with 24 of the 26 Black women who I interviewed—I found out that televised content had also played a central part in the lives of most of them at some stage, particularly media depictions of Black women that they came across as children.

When interviewed, Plantain Baby, who is in her twenties, is an artist, and is based in England, wistfully reflected on representations of Black women and girls in media that she encountered as a child in Britain:

> I remember growing up and like, watching TV...there was a lot of like African American programmes, but of the Black British ones that were here...I remember *Cleopatra*. *Cleopatra* was, I feel like...the peak representation on TV to do with Black British girlhood...that's it! And that was a long time ago, there's no DVD, there's no reference, there's nothing...it just like, came and passed. I remember watching *Cleopatra* in the mornings 'cause they do reruns. I remember watching it on ITV when they did reruns...and they were three Black girls...I think they were from Birmingham...these three Black girls, and I thought they were so cool...and then okay, Naomi Campbell...this Black unapologetic supermodel, I remember...from Brixton...because it felt like...not like I knew her, but it was like...my cousins. Naomi Campbell, I can see her in my auntie, I can see her in my cousins...and it was something good to see all the time...it doesn't have to be an exact representation of you, but it was just seeing Blackness as much as possible, because we do exist, we are here...there were even some shows on BBC... there was this show on TV...*Kerching!*...and like the characters, the older sister and the sister's friends...that kind of TV show doesn't exist [now].

Plantain Baby also spoke fondly of the British subscription television channel, Trouble, which operated from 1997 to 2009 and featured many shows which included Black leading roles. Trouble was mentioned and remembered by 20 of the women who I interviewed—all of whom were under the age of 30 years old when we spoke, and who may be typified as 'millennials', by some. Among the women who spoke of Trouble fondly was Annie, who is in her late teens and is an undergraduate student based in England. Annie spoke about the notable part that Trouble played in her childhood media experiences:

> When I was younger we didn't always have Sky...my mother didn't let us watch TV much, but they were showing *Fresh Prince of Bel-Air*...but when we did get Sky we saw that there were channels like Trouble, and Trouble did a good job, they called it 'urban' but there were quite a few shows where there were Black female leads, or even just Black females on the show, like *My Wife and Kids*, *Girlfriends*, *Eve*, there was *Sister Sister*,

Moesha...but I was also aware, especially around aged 14 years old, that there are not really many Black females [on TV], especially in the UK. It's bad. It's really, really bad...and even in the shows like *Kidulthood* or whatever, the Black females will be shown by 'mixed-race' females, but by then I was already finding my shows online to watch...so yeah, I guess I did watch a lot [of television programmes with Black women in] them, but I guess I sought them out. I liked it [Trouble] and was always drawn to it because I just saw myself, and I guess with Trouble TV it was often comedy...and like, *Friends* was all the rage and I just didn't find it funny at all, but with the stuff on Trouble I could just relate to it, even stuff that they made light of, you had kind of seen it happen with your mum or cousins...could enjoy it more and I'd really get the jokes.

As Annie's comments touch on, due to colourism and co-dependent anti-Blackness, often when Black women feature on-screen in Britain it tends to be images and the experiences of 'mixed-race' and light-skinned Black women that are foregrounded, and at the exclusion of dark-skinned Black women, or who are depicted in comparatively derogatory and degrading ways.

For many of the women who I spoke to who had grown up watching Trouble TV, it had represented a nostalgic 'golden era' of media depictions of Black women of different shades, yet, had still featured shows that contained colourist messages, plots, and casting and production decisions that targeted dark-skinned Black women in oppressive ways. Many of the shows that were available on Trouble were also based on heteronormative narratives concerning heterosexual romance, marriage, and idealised family life—resulting in the hyper-visibility of on-screen depictions of heterosexual Black women, in comparison to the lack of depictions of lesbian, bisexual, and queer Black women.

Other comments about the colourism that was apparent in shows on Trouble include the following words in reference to *The Fresh Prince of Bel-Air*, which were said by Nymeria who is an artist in her twenties in Scotland:

> The real aunt Viv! The real aunt Viv...it's funny 'cause they could have just picked another dark-skinned Black woman [to play her once the original actor—Janet Hubert—was reportedly fired from the show], but they made the decision to make her lighter-skinned, but the woman who played *real* aunt Viv was amaaaaazing!...I realised when I was re-watching it how much she meant to me.

When speaking about the specific significance of Trouble TV for some Black girls and women in Britain, Nymeria said:

> ...the funny thing is I talk about that stuff with my white friends [now] and they have no idea what I'm on about because they didn't consume that media...they didn't feel the need to...when I'm like 'do you remember *My Wife and Kids*?', they're like 'no', everyone remembers *Fresh Prince of Bel-Air* but hardly anybody was aware of the Black TV on Trouble and I was sooo glad that existed...I still think that *Moesha* was like my fave...all I remember was watching this and feeling a sense of 'I need to watch this'.

Some of the comments of another woman who I interviewed, named Rachel, who is in her twenties and is a recent graduate based in England, were very similar to Nymeria's remarks about the significant role of Trouble TV in the childhood of some Black women in Britain:

> I was in my own little world of Rachel growing up...it was only when like, I came to uni and started talking to other people [about Trouble TV], and they were like, 'what are you talking about? I've never heard of that before'

Trouble was a relatively short-lived television channel that has an especially strong sentimental value for Black women in Britain who had access to it, grew up as children watching Trouble TV shows, and eventually witnessed the channel's decline. While Trouble offered media depictions of Black women that were often absent from many mass-media contexts in Britain, within the roster of shows that it featured there was still a dearth of depictions of Black women *in* and *from* Britain. When considering how Trouble influenced the childhood media experiences of some Black women in Britain, it is important to recognise that many of the shows that aired on the channel and featured Black casts were North American—and as a result, may be interpreted as being part of what anthropologist Jacqueline Nassy Brown refers to as 'discursive forays into "black America"' (Nassy Brown 1998, p. 291) in Britain, and which can impact the identities of Black people (t)here.

Not all women who I spoke to were of a similar age or had access to Trouble TV as children, including Amoke, who is in her forties, works in the public sector and is based in Scotland. Amoke identified many restrictive stereotypes that she feels television depictions of Black women in Britain promote. Amoke, who moved to Scotland from a city in West

Africa about a decade ago, and said the move 'was meant to be temporary actually', discussed perceived 'improvements' to the media representation of Black women in Britain:

> My thoughts? It's different from when I first came here [Scotland]. Actually, looking back to then, I didn't even look for them [representations of Black women], probably because subconsciously I didn't even expect to see them, but now I think there is more...in terms of visibility of them, not necessarily what they do...you see more Black and minority ethnic women on tele...one of them is Charlene White on the 6 o'clock news and maybe 10 o'clock news and I think *that's* just fantastic, and one in the morning, like GMTV as well...so there are more women I think. I still don't think...I don't have any statistics, but I don't think it's nearly enough to make some sort of impression on a younger person, but as somebody who has lived through when there was even *nothing*...I actually...I don't remember when I first came. I was never a big tele person, but initially I remember this woman in *EastEnders*. I think she is still there...I don't actually remember her name but she's been there a long time and her little family...it's not...not that she's a negative image...what she does, but...she doesn't stand out as someone you admire, so she's...yeah, she's just a 'problem family' and switching from relationship to relationship, but she's there...it's only now that they are actually looking at them and what they do.

Amoke made remarks that encompass how issues concerning generational, regional, and diasporic identity can impact the media expectations and experiences of Black women in Britain—such as their perceptions of the extent to which on-screen depictions of Black women have changed or 'improved', as Amoke put it. Although media depictions of Black women on Trouble played a central role in the childhood experiences of some Black women in Britain—including Plantain Baby, Nymeria, Rachel, and myself—, as is indicated by similarities and differences between the perspectives of the women who I interviewed, this is not the case for all.

Amoke was one of several mothers who I spoke to. Others, including Poppy, shared experiences that were reflective of how 'parental attempts to (re)mediate the Black identities of their children may involve them drawing on a global range of marketplace symbolic resources' (Sobande 2018, p. 45) in an effort to defy mainstream media messages that promote 'ideological notions of inferior African "otherness"' (Bonsu 2009, p. 1). The mothers who I interviewed made comments that are illustrative of Black 'parents' awareness of the scope for media representations to influence perceptions of their children, as well as their children's self-perceptions' (Sobande 2018, p. 43).

The experiences of Black people in Britain took a 'dramatic and definitive shape during the 1970s, leading in turn to an unprecedented period of Black-British creativity during the early to mid 1980s' (Chambers 2017, p. xiii). In the twenty-first century, the creative, collective and consciousness-raising endeavours of Black people in Britain continue to flourish (Rae 2020), sometimes in ways mediated by digital communication and marketplace activity. Britain's contemporary media landscape is one within which Black women are carving out spaces and producing platforms and media outlets of their own.

When speaking to Ruby, who is in her twenties, is based in England and has experience of working in the media industry in Britain, she said the following:

> …a lot of the time when we talk about imagery of Black women, it's always very American centric…I don't really know why that's the case, 'cause I think that British drama is quite forward thinking with sci-fi stuff and dystopias, comedy dramas…it's so strange that when I think of Black women on TV I think of Kerry Washington and Shonda Rhimes…we didn't really think that we had the platform to share our own voices, or we didn't see representations of ourselves…then if we do see them, a lot of the time they're 'mixed-race'…I don't see many Black women in British TV or film and when I do see them, they're just throw away characters. A friend of mine created a little report on Black women for a channel and it had like 20 something million views shared, and they said as soon as the idea was pitched, they knew it would pick up, because Black women share and create the most content about themselves…when we create content, and when I say 'we', I mean like…young media savvy Black women and women of colour, we create content for *us*, by *us*, which is great…but sometimes it feels like we're just regurgitating the same message to people who already think the same…your own circle.

The depiction of Black women in media in Britain has changed in some ways throughout history, including as a result of the rise of social media and digital communication platforms. However, there are striking elements of Black women's media experiences which seem to be steadfast. Among these is the scarcity of Black women's substantial leadership presence amid many media institutions and production processes—with Black people's involvement in British television as actors, writers and producers only slowly starting to increase with significance in the 1980s.

Furthermore, due to the intersections of anti-Black racism, sexism and other types of entwined structural oppression, when working in the media industry, and many other industries, Black women in Britain are likely to face difficulties associated with precarious work which 'refers to all forms of insecure, contingent, flexible work – from illegalized, casualized and temporary employment, to homeworking, piecework and freelancing' (Gill and Pratt 2008, p. 3). Consequently, even when able to enter media and cultural industry-related work environments, Black women in Britain commonly face insurmountable structural barriers connected to a lack of job security, insufficient pay, and an absence of organisational support—linked to intersecting oppressions.

Ruby emphasised the deficiency of television representations of Black women in Britain and commented on the fact that when Black women are represented it is in a very narrow and stereotypical way, including as part of content that feels as though it has been created for the viewing pleasure of people who in fact perpetuate the anti-Black types of oppression that Black people face. Many of those who I interviewed discussed their efforts to avoid certain media outlets which they feel distribute stereotypical images of Black women and uphold racist and sexist ideologies. This notion was part of why most of those who I spoke to dismiss the British Broadcasting Corporation (BBC), as well as various mainstream print magazines (Sobande et al. 2019)—particularly due to their awareness of the fact that '[m]edia production and distribution systems remain primarily in the hands of white, elite men; and global information and capital flows still largely privilege their views, preoccupations, and economic goals' (Carter et al. 2014, p. 1). When I spoke to Ralph-Angel, who is in her thirties and is a photographer and graduate in Scotland, she emphasised this point (Sobande et al. 2019) when discussing why she 'just stopped watching the BBC and CNN and other stuff...all this mainstream white media'.

Ruby stressed the need for the media to depict Black women with more nuance and to account for their differences, including those shaped by colourism (Adegoke 2019; Amoah 2019; Gabriel 2007; Tate 2009, 2017a, b). The spirit of the words of singer-songwriter and consummate creative Solange Knowles when accepting her first Grammy Award in 2016 captures the sentiments of some of what was said by those who I interviewed:

> I think that visual art, in all aspects, are super important to me…creating strong visual representation of not only myself but, again, Black women, and getting to see us as avant-garde beings in a world that sometimes puts us in a box is really important to me.

Many Black women do not simply want to see more images and representation of Black women in the media. Instead, there is a demand for more of an expansive range of depictions, produced by Black women, for them, and as part of media and creativity that spans genres and generations.

REGIONALITY AND RURALITY

Studies of the relationship between Blackness and commercial culture have elucidated how the experiences of Black people in different parts of the world are remediated. In the case of sociologist Herman Gray's (2004) work, there is exploration of 'processes by which questions about the American racial order – and, within it, blackness–are constructed, reproduced, and challenged' (p. 1). While writing such as that of Gray's (2004) has illuminated some of the intricacies of how national politics and understandings of race and Blackness are placed together within marketplace contexts, the workings of regional dynamics and the specifics of local settings have less commonly played a core part in research related to race, Blackness, media, and cultural spheres.

As hill (2019) succinctly puts it, 'representation of local news from smaller regions and towns beyond the central belt [in Scotland] or main cities still struggle to make it into new independent media'. This observation is also applicable to other parts of Britain where there is a greater amount of monetary, political, and societal focus on media content stemming from large cities, in comparison to material that originates in smaller areas. As is conveyed by the scholarship of Joy White (2019) on 'Growing Up in "The Ends": Identity, Place and Belonging in an Urban East London Neighbourhood', experiences of Black life in Britain are affected by the local surroundings that people find themselves living in, as well as the wider national setting that they are tied to.

Recognising how regional factors affect the lives of Black people, in videos for BBC The Social, writer Tomiwa Folorunso (2018a, b) discusses the experience of growing up Black and Scottish—affirming the need to acknowledge similarities and differences between the lives of Black women across various parts of Britain. When taking into consideration such perspectives, it is clear that meaningful efforts to learn about the media representation and experiences of Black women in Britain require an understanding of national and regional dynamics—beyond simply distinguishing between England, Scotland, Wales, and Northern Ireland. In addition, there is a need to scrutinise the prevalence of high-profile media from capital cities and the comparatively constrained visibility and funding available to media outlets, practitioners, creatives and freelancers in small towns and rural areas.

Patterns of migration and Britain's involvement in the transatlantic enslavement of Black people have resulted in the distinct presence of Black communities in cities including London, Liverpool, Cardiff, Manchester, Birmingham, and Glasgow (Bryan et al. 2018). However, Black women are not only based in large cities in Britain, as is reflected in the experiences of some of the women who I interviewed—including Lucy, who is in her twenties, is a creative performer and works in hospitality part-time in Scotland. Lucy voiced frustration concerning a lack of adequate media depictions of Black women who are from parts of Britain other than England. Lucy, who identifies as Scottish, spoke of 'the Scottish thing' being really important, and never getting to 'see anyone on TV who looked like us, and speaks like us'. When thinking about how significant it would have been to have had access to depictions of Black women in Scotland on TV when she was younger, Lucy paused before saying 'oh my god, it would have been the most amazing thing ever!'.

In the case of another woman who I interviewed, named Bobino, who is in her thirties, much of her life has been spent living in a rural part of England:

> …somewhere with generated electricity, which means that the electricity goes off. There have been no neighbours, so it's fairly remote. And my mother's mother would make video recordings from films that were on television.

Bobino was one of two women I interviewed who spoke of living in a remote and rural area, where they were one of very few Black girls and women, if not, the only, Black girl or woman for miles. Bobino's experience of growing up without watching television and with limited access to electricity indicates how the different regional locations that Black women in Britain live in can influence their media experiences, as can other aspects of their home life and circumstances. Such a point is consistent with research regarding the digital experiences of Black and Latino youth in the US which highlights how regardless of 'living in a hyperconnected world where physical distance is often characterized as immaterial, geography – or more precisely, where people live – still matters' (Watkins et al. 2018, p. 4). The experiences of Black women in Britain such as Bobino are a reminder of stark inequalities concerning Black women's access to the internet and televised media, including within countries where it is often mistakenly assumed that all people can simply go online or watch television at the touch of a button in their home.

Concluding Thoughts

The media experiences of Black women in Britain have changed over the decades but among what has remained consistent are struggles against their limited and derogatory depiction in 'controlling images' (Hill Collins 2000, p. 114) that are 'externally defined' (ibid.) by others. Constant challenges that such women face include contending with hostile and racist media institution environments when in pursuit of industry work, and the prospect of dealing with discriminatory backlash from the public when featuring on-screen and becoming hyper-visible in the media. As the words of Poppy indicate, oppressive responses to the depiction of different Black women in Britain in media can be the result of interlocking structural factors including, but not limited to, anti-Black racism, Islamophobia, xenophobia, sexism, and misogyny.

Since the days of events and collective work in the 1980s led by Black women in Britain concerning their media experiences and material conditions, increased availability and accessibility of digital devices and content-creation processes has resulted in new opportunities for Black women to relatively autonomously produce media, depict themselves, and generate discourse that counters dominant narratives. As is explored in detail in the next two chapters, attempts to counter how Black women in Britain have been systemically discriminated against within the media, creative and cultural industries, as well as society in general, include the digital efforts of Black women who collectively create together and build new avenues and activities to widely share their writing, work, and political organising.

Notes

1. The term 'BME' which stands for Black and Minority Ethnic is one which rightly continues to be critiqued, including due to its use often involving a lack of specificity concerning racial and ethnic identities and experiences; especially at the expense of understandings of the lives of Black people of African descent and the particularities of anti-Blackness that they encounter. For this reason, the term 'BME' only features in this book as part of discussion of prior writing and research that makes use of it in connection to the lives of Black women.
2. The Black women who were interviewed include individuals who were born in Britain, as well as those who are migrants and refugees. At the time of the interviews, everyone resided in either Scotland or England. Those who were interviewed include individuals with different class backgrounds and socio-economic experiences, however, most had studied at college or university level. Among the Black women who were interviewed were individuals who are bisexual, heterosexual, lesbian and queer. Nobody specifically spoke about being cis, trans* or genderqueer, so the particularities of Black women's gender identities are not focused on in detail in this book but there is recognition of how Black trans* women and genderqueer individuals are most structurally oppressed and face specific forms of harassment, abuse, and violence that Black cis women do not.

References

Adegoke, Yomi. (2019). 'Dark skinned women are now being celebrated, but don't blame us for scepticism.' *Metro*. Last modified 23 August, https://metro.co.uk/2019/08/23/dark-skinned-women-are-now-being-celebrated-but-dont-blame-us-for-scepticism-10619341. Accessed 5 November 2019.

Adewunmi, Bim. (2012). 'Why Black British drama is going online, not on TV.' *The Guardian*. Last modified 2 July, https://www.theguardian.com/world/2012/jul/02/black-british-tv-drama-online. Accessed 15 September 2016.

Akpan, Paula. (2019). 'How the stories of Black women in the UK are being reclaimed.' *Refinery29*. Last modified 10 October, https://www.refinery29.com/en-gb/black-women-history-uk. Accessed 15 October 2019.

Alabanza, Travis. (2018). 'Dear Naomi: We need to say her name.' *gal-dem*. Last modified 28 March, http://gal-dem.com/silence-failing-naomi-hersi. Accessed 5 April 2018.

Allen, Kim & Hollingworth, Sumi. (2013). '"Sticky subjects" or "cosmopolitan creatives"? Social class, place and urban young people's aspirations for work in the knowledge economy.' *Urban Studies* 50(3): 499–517. https://journals.sagepub.com/doi/abs/10.1177/0042098012468901.

Amoah, Susuana. (2019). '#NoShade: A critical analysis of digital influencer activism against shadeism in the beauty industry.' *Academia.edu*, https://www.academia.edu/39881809/NoShade_A_Critical_Analysis_of_Digital_Influencer_Activism_Against_Shadeism_in_the_Beauty_Industry. Accessed 30 July 2019.

Bailey, Moya. (2020). 'A radical reckoning: A Black woman's racial revenge in *Black Mirror's* "Black Museum".' *Feminist Media Studies*. https://doi.org/10.1080/14680777.2020.1736120.

Banet-Weiser, Sarah. (2018). *Empowered: Popular Feminism and Popular Misogyny*. Durham and London: Duke University Press.

Bassel, Leah & Emejulu, Akwugo. (2017). *Minority Women and Austerity: Survival and Resistance in France and Britain*. Bristol: Policy Press.

Benjamin, Ruha. (2019). *Race After Technology: Abolitionist Tools for the New Jim Code*. Cambridge and Medford, MA: Polity Press.

Benson, Michaela & Lewis, Chantelle. (2019). 'Brexit, British people of colour in the EU-27 and everyday racism in Britain and Europe.' *Ethnic and Racial Studies* 42(13): 2211–2228. https://www.tandfonline.com/doi/full/10.1080/01419870.2019.1599134.

Bentil, Jade. (Forthcoming, 2021). *Rebel Citizen: A History of Black Women Living, Loving and Resisting*. London: Penguin/Allen Lane.

Bishop, Marla. (1987). 'Black women and invisibility.' *Spare Rib*, Issue 1987 (177): 32.

Black Rights (UK). (1988). *Black People, Human Rights and The Media*. London: Black Rights (UK) with the assistance of the Commission for Racial Equality.

Bobo, Jacqueline. (1995). *Black Women as Cultural Readers*. New York: Columbia University Press.

Bobo, Jacqueline. (ed.) (2001). *Black Feminist Cultural Criticism*. Malden, MA: Blackwell.

Bonsu, Samuel K. (2009). 'Colonial images in global times: Consumer interpretations of Africa and Africans in advertising.' *Consumption Markets & Cultures* 12(1): 1–25. https://www.tandfonline.com/doi/abs/10.1080/10253860802560789.

Brinkhurst-Cuff, Charlie. (ed.) (2018). *Mother Country: Real Stories of the Windrush Children*. London: Headline.

Brinkhurst-Cuff, Charlie. (2019). 'Joy Morgan can be laid to rest, but more needs to be uncovered about her murder.' *gal-dem*. Last modified 11 October, http://gal-dem.com/joy-morgan-can-be-laid-to-rest-but-more-needs-to-be-uncovered-about-her-murder. Accessed 15 October 2019.

Bryan, Beverley, Dadzie, Stella & Scafe, Suzanne. (1985). *The Heart of the Race: Black Women's Lives in Britain*. London: Virago.
Bryan, Beverley, Dadzie, Stella & Scafe, Suzanne. (2018). *The Heart of the Race: Black Women's Lives in Britain* (2nd ed.). London: Verso.
Carter, Cynthia, Steiner, Linda & McLaughlin, Lisa. (eds.) (2014). *The Routledge Companion to Media and Gender*. New York: Routledge.
Chambers, Eddie. (2017). *Roots and Culture: Cultural Politics in the Making of Black Britain*. London: I.B. Tauris.
Chambers, Nadine. (2019). 'Sometimes clocks turn back for us to move forward: Reflections on Black and Indigenous geographies.' *Canada and Beyond: A Journal of Canadian Literary and Cultural Studies* 8(2019): 22–39. http://dx.doi.org/10.33776/candb.v8i1.4566.
Cole, Marverine. (2018). 'The "strong Black woman" stereotype is harming our mental health.' *The Guardian*. Last Modified 20 July, https://www.theguardian.com/commentisfree/2018/jul/20/strong-black-woman-stereotype-mental-health-depression-self-harm. Accessed 15 September 2018.
Crockett, David. (2008). 'Marketing blackness: How advertisers use race to sell products.' *Journal of Consumer Culture* 8(2): 245–268. https://journals.sagepub.com/doi/10.1177/1469540508090088.
Cruel Ironies Collective. (2019). 'Cruel ironies: The afterlife of Black womxn's intervention.' In *To Exist Is to Resist: Black Feminism in Europe*, edited by Akwugo Emejulu & Francesca Sobande, pp. 181–194. London: Pluto Press.
Dabiri, Emma. (2013). 'Who stole all the Black women from Britain?' *Media Diversified*. Last modified 5 November, https://mediadiversified.org/2013/11/05/who-stole-all-the-black-women-from-britain. Accessed 15 May 2018.
Davis, Angela Y. (1981). *Women, Race & Class*. New York: Random House.
Dawes, Laina. (2012). *What Are You Doing Here? A Black Woman's Life and Liberation in Heavy Metal*. Brooklyn, NY: Bazillion Points.
Emejulu, Akwugo. (2016). 'On the hideous whiteness of Brexit: "Let us be honest about our past and our present if we truly seek to dismantle white supremacy".' *Verso*. Last modified 28 June, https://www.versobooks.com/blogs/2733-on-the-hideous-whiteness-of-brexit-let-us-be-honest-about-our-past-and-our-present-if-we-truly-seek-to-dismantle-white-supremacy. Accessed 30 June 2016.
Emejulu, Akwugo & Sobande, Francesca. (eds.) (2019). *To Exist is to Resist: Black Feminism in Europe*. London: Pluto Press.
European Women's Lobby (from the European Forum of Left Feminists). (1995). *Confronting The Fortress: Black and Migrant Women in the European Union*. European Parliament.
Folorunso, Tomiwa. (2018a). 'Growing up Black in Scotland [video].' *BBC The Social*. Last modified 15 October, https://www.youtube.com/watch?reload=9&v=WCzK2JkIodE. Accessed 9 June 2019.

Folorunso, Tomiwa. (2018b). 'Learning about Black Scottish history! [video].' *BBC The Social.* Last modified 29 October, https://www.youtube.com/watch?v=EixjHZ9GaEk. Accessed 9 June 2019.

Folorunso, Tomiwa. (2019). 'Scotland is not this anti-racist utopia that we pretend it is.' *The Herald.* Last modified 28 October, https://www.heraldscotland.com/news/17997473.scotland-not-anti-racist-utopia-pretend. Accessed 9 November 2019.

Gabriel, Deborah. (2007). *Layers of Blackness: Colourism in the African Diaspora.* London: Imani Media Ltd.

Gabriel, Deborah. (2016). 'Blogging while Black, British and female: A critical study on discursive activism.' *Information, Communication & Society* 19(11): 1622–1635. https://doi.org/10.1080/1369118X.2016.1146784.

Gammage, Marquita Marie. (2016). *Representations of Black Women in the Media: The Damnation of Black Womanhood.* New York: Routledge.

Gill, Rosalind & Pratt, Andy. (2008). 'In the social factory?: Immaterial labour, precariousness and cultural work.' *Theory, Culture & Society* 25(7–8): 1–30. https://journals.sagepub.com/doi/10.1177/0263276408097794.

Gilroy, Paul. (1987). *'There Ain't No Black in the Union Jack': The Cultural Politics of Race and Nation.* London: Unwin Hyman.

Glissant, Édouard. (1997). *Poetics of Relation.* Ann Arbor: University of Michigan Press.

Gray, Herman. (2004). *Watching Race: Television and the Struggle for Blackness.* Minneapolis: University of Minnesota Press.

Gray, Herman. (2015). 'The feel of life: Resonance, race, and representation.' *International Journal of Communication* 9: 1108–1119. https://ijoc.org/index.php/ijoc/article/view/2238.

Grier, Sonya A., Thomas, Kevin D. & Johnson, Guillaume D. (2019). 'Re-imagining the marketplace: Addressing race in academic marketing research.' *Consumption Markets & Culture* 22(1): 91–100. https://doi.org/10.1080/10253866.2017.1413800.

Hall, Stuart. (ed.) (1997). *Representation: Cultural Representations and Signifying Practices.* London: Sage in association with The Open University.

Hall, Stuart. (2001). 'Constituting an archive.' *Third Text* 15(54): 89–92. https://doi.org/10.1080/09528820108576903.

Hall, Stuart, Evans, Jessica & Nixon, Sean. (eds.) (2012). *Representations: Cultural Representations and Signifying Practices* (2nd ed.). London: Sage.

Hesmondhalgh, David & Saha, Anamik. (2013). 'Race, ethnicity, and cultural production.' *Popular Communication: The International Journal of Media and Culture* 11(3): 179–195. https://doi.org/10.1080/15405702.2013.810068.

hill, layla-roxanne. (2017). 'Blackout—Why aren't Black British women treated fairly in the media?' Last modified 30 March, http://nujscotland.org.uk/

2017/03/30/news-blackout-why-arent-black-british-women-treated-fairly-in-the-media. Accessed 30 June 2018.

hill, layla-roxanne. (2019). 'Know the media, be the media, change the media.' *Bella Caledonia*. Last modified 29 September, https://bellacaledonia.org.uk/2019/09/29/know-the-media-be-the-media-change-the-media. Accessed 3 October 2019.

Hill Collins, Patricia. (2000). *Black Feminist Thought: Knowledge, Consciousness, and the Politics of Empowerment* (2nd ed.). New York and London: Routledge.

Hill Collins, Patricia & Bilge, Sirma. (2016). *Intersectionality*. Cambridge: Polity Press.

Hirsch, Afua. (2018). 'Glossies so white: The data that reveals the problem with British magazine covers.' *The Guardian*. Last modified 10 April, https://www.theguardian.com/media/2018/apr/10/glossy-magazine-covers-too-white-models-black-ethnic-minority. Accessed 20 June 2018.

Hobson, Janell. (2008). 'Digital whiteness, primitive blackness: Racializing the "digital divide" in film and new media.' *Feminist Media Studies* 8(2): 111–126. https://doi.org/10.1080/00220380801980467.

hooks, bell. (1992). *Black Looks: Race and Representation*. Boston: South End Press.

hooks, bell. (2009). *Reel to Real: Race, Class and Sex at the Movies*. New York: Routledge.

Jackson, Sarah J., Bailey, Moya & Foucault Welles, Brooke. (2017). '#GirlsLikeUs: Trans advocacy and community building online.' *New Media & Society* 20(5): 1868–1888. https://doi.org/10.1177/1461444817709276.

Jackson, Sarah J., Bailey, Moya & Foucault Welles, Brooke. (2020). *#HashtagActivism: Networks of Race and Gender Justice*. Cambridge, MA and London: MIT Press.

Jameela, Maryam. (Forthcoming, 2020). '"Violence, above all, is what maintains the breach": Racial categorisation and the flattening of difference.' In *Black Film British Cinema II*, edited by Clive Nwonka & Anamik Saha. Cambridge: MIT Press.

Johnson, Azeezat. (2017). '"You're Othered here and you're Othered there": Centring the clothing practices of Black Muslim Women in Britain.' PhD Thesis, University of Sheffield. http://etheses.whiterose.ac.uk/id/eprint/18428.

Johnson, Azeezat, Joseph-Salisbury, Remi & Kamunge, Beth. (eds.) (2018). *The Fire Now: Anti-Racist Scholarship in Times of Explicit Racial Violence*. London: Zed Books.

Johnson, Guillaume D., Thomas, Kevin D., Harrison, Anthony K. & Grier, Sonya A. (eds.) (2019). *Race in the Marketplace: Crossing Critical Boundaries*. Cham: Palgrave Macmillan.
Joseph, Ralina L. (2019). *Postracial Resistance: Black Women, Media, and the Uses of Strategic Ambiguity*. New York: New York University Press.
Kanai, Akane. (2019). *Gender and Relatability in Digital Culture: Managing Affect, Intimacy and Value*. Cham: Palgrave Macmillan.
Kyeremateng, Tobi. (2019). 'Why the obsession with "breaking stereotypes" is harming Black people.' *gal-dem*. Last modified 25 September, http://gal-dem.com/why-the-obsession-with-breaking-stereotypes-is-harming-black-people. Accessed 29 September 2019.
Larasi, Marai. (2019). 'Foreword.' In *This Is Us: Black British Women and Girls*, curated by Kafayat Okanlawon, pp. 5–9. London: Break the Habit Press.
Lewis, Gail. (1993). 'Black Women's Employment and the British Economy.' In *Inside Babylon: The Caribbean Diaspora in Britain*, edited by Winston James & Clive Harris, pp. 73–96. London: Verso.
Lewis, Gail. (2000). *'Race', Gender, Social Welfare: Encounters in a Postcolonial Society*. Cambridge: Polity Press.
Lewis, Gail & Hemmings, Clare. (2019). '"Where might we go if we dare": Moving beyond the "thick, suffocating fog of whiteness" in feminism.' *Feminist Theory* 20(4). 106–121. https://doi.org/10.1177/1464700119871220.
Linton, Samara & Walcott, Rianna. (eds.) (2018). *The Colour of Madness: Exploring BAME Mental Health in the UK*. Edinburgh: Stirling Publishing.
Lorde, Audre. (1988). *A Burst of Light*. New York: Firebrand Books.
Maylor, Uvanney. (2009). 'What is the meaning of "Black"? Researching "Black" respondents.' *Ethnic and Racial Studies* 32(2): 369–387. https://www.tandfonline.com/doi/abs/10.1080/01419870802196773.
Media Diversified. (ed.) (2016). *From the Lines of Dissent*. London: Out-Spoken Press.
Melancon, Trimiko. (2014). *Unbought and Unbossed: Transgressive Black Women, Sexuality, and Representation*. Philadelphia: Temple University Press.
Morris, Valerie. (1986). 'MITAG: Minorities Information Technology Awareness Group'. In March 1986 Issue (27) of the Greater London Council Women's Committee Bulletin, pp. 39–40.
Morrison, Toni. (2017). *The Origin of Others*. Cambridge, MA and London: Harvard University Press.
Nassy Brown, Jacqueline. (1998). 'Black Liverpool, Black America, and the gendering of diasporic space.' *Cultural Anthropology* 13(3): 291–325. https://doi.org/10.1525/can.1998.13.3.291.
Ngcobo, Lauretta. (ed.) (1987). *Let It Be Told: Essays by Black Women in Britain*. London: Pluto Press.

Noble, Safiya Umoja. (2018). *Algorithms of Oppression: How Search Engines Reinforce Racism.* New York: New York University Press.
Noble, Safiya Umoja & Tynes, Brendesha M. (eds.) (2016). *The Intersectional Internet: Race, Sex, Class, and Culture Online.* New York: Peter Lang.
Obasi, Chijioke. (2019). 'Africanist Sista-hood in Britain: Creating our own pathways.' In *To Exist Is to Resist: Black Feminism in Europe*, edited by Akwugo Emejulu & Francesca Sobande, pp. 229–242. London: Pluto Press.
Okolosie, Lola. (2018). 'Preface.' In *The Heart of the Race: The Lives of Black Women in Britain* (2nd ed.), written by Bryan, Beverley, Dadzie, Stella & Scafe, Suzanne. London: Verso.
Olumide, Eunice. (2019). 'I will not stop talking about the racism I face even if it means I lose my job.' *Metro*. Last modified 14 May, https://metro.co.uk/2019/05/14/i-will-not-stop-talking-about-the-racism-i-face-even-if-it-means-i-lose-my-job-9467895. Accessed 2 June 2019.
Omonira-Oyekanmi, Rebecca. (2010). 'The injustice of indefinite detention.' *The Guardian*. Last modified 5 October, https://www.theguardian.com/commentisfree/libertycentral/2010/oct/05/british-immigration-removal-centres-injustice. Accessed 8 October 2019.
Omonira-Oyekanmi, Rebecca. (2016). 'Remembering Sarah Reed.' *Open Democracy*. Last Modified 13 February, https://www.opendemocracy.net/en/shine-a-light/remembering-sarah-reed. Accessed 19 February 2019.
Otele, Olivette. (2017). 'History of slavery, sites of memory, and identity politics in contemporary Britain.' In *A Stain on Our Past: Slavery and Memory*, edited by Abdoulaye Gueye & Johann Michel, pp. 189–210. Trenton: Africa World Press.
Otele, Olivette. (2019). 'We need to talk about slavery's impact on all of us.' *The Guardian*. Last modified 9 November, https://www.theguardian.com/commentisfree/2019/nov/09/slavery-impact-trauma-history. Accessed 18 November 2019.
Owusu, Melz. (2018). 'Decolonising the academy: A movement without borders.' *Medium*. Last modified 12 November, https://medium.com/@melz.artist/decolonising-the-academy-a-movement-without-borders-7a25c071db6e. Accessed 4 January 2019.
Palmer, Lisa Amanda. (2011). 'The politics of loving blackness in the UK.' PhD Thesis. University of Birmingham. https://etheses.bham.ac.uk/id/eprint/1508/. Accessed 7 January 2018.
Perry, Kennetta Hammond. (2016). *London is the Place for Me: Black Britons, Citizenship, and the Politics of Race.* New York: Oxford University Press.

Rae, Mandla. (2020). 'Creative conversations: Black women artists making and doing—Institute for Black Atlantic Research, Preston.' *Corridor8*. Last modified 29 February, https://corridor8.co.uk/article/black-women-artists-making-and-doing. Accessed 29 February 2020.

Scott, David. (2016). Cited in Scott, David, James, Erica Moiah & Cunningham, Nijah. *Caribbean Queer Visualities*, pp. 3–5. Small Axe.

Sharpe, Christina. (2016). *In the Wake: On Blackness and Being*. Durham and London: Duke University Press.

Sims, Jennifer Patrice & Njaka, Chinelo L. (2019). *Mixed-Race in the US and UK: Comparing the Past, Present, and Future*. Bingley: Emerald.

Sobande, Francesca. (2017). 'Watching me watching you: Black women in Britain on YouTube.' *European Journal of Cultural Studies* 20(6): 655–671. https://doi.org/10.1177/1367549417733001.

Sobande, Francesca. (2018). 'Managing media as parental race-work: (Re)mediating children's Black identities.' In *Consumer Culture Theory: Research in Consumer Behavior*, Vol. 19, edited by Samantha N. N. Cross, Cecilia Ruvalcaba, Alladi Venkatesh & Russell W. Belk, pp. 37–53. Bingley: Emerald.

Sobande, Francesca. (2019a). 'Memes, digital remix culture and (re)mediating British politics and public life.' *IPPR Progressive Review* 26(2): 151–160. https://onlinelibrary.wiley.com/doi/abs/10.1111/newe.12155.

Sobande, Francesca. (2019b). 'Woke-washing: "Intersectional" femvertising and branding "woke" bravery.' *European Journal of Marketing*, Vol. Ahead-of-print No. ahead-of-print. https://doi.org/10.1108/EJM-02-2019-0134.

Sobande, Francesca, Fearfull, Anne & Brownlie, Douglas. (2019). 'Resisting media marginalisation: Black women's digital content and collectivity.' *Consumption Markets & Culture*. doi.org/https://doi.org/10.1080/10253866.2019.1571491.

Spare Rib. (1984a). 'Black women & media conference.' *Spare Rib*, Issue 1984(143): 18.

Spare Rib. (1984b). 'We're here...Black women meet.' *Spare Rib*, Issue 1984(144): 21.

Spare Rib. (1992). 'Computer hazards.' *Spare Rib*, Issue 1992(234): 58.

Sulter, Maud. (1985). *As a Blackwoman*. London: Akira.

Sulter, Maud. (1986). 'Surveying the scene: Writings by women of African and Asian descent.' In March 1986 Issue (27) of the Greater London Council Women's Committee Bulletin, pp. 28–29.

Tate, Shirley Anne. (2009). *Black Beauty: Aesthetics, Stylization, Politics*. Farnham: Ashgate Publishing.

Tate, Shirley Anne. (2017a). *The Governmentality of Black Beauty Shame: Discourse, Iconicity and Resistance*. Basingstoke: Palgrave Macmillan.

Tate, Shirley Anne. (2017b). 'Skin: Post-feminist bleaching culture and the political vulnerability of blackness.' In *Aesthetic Labour: Rethinking Beauty Politics in Neoliberalism*, edited by Ana Sofia Elias, Rosalind Gill & Christina Scharff, pp. 199–213. Basingstoke: Palgrave Macmillan.
The Brixton Black Women's Group and the Organisation for Women of African and Asian Descent. (2017). *Black Women Organising*. London: Past Tense.
The Greater London Council Women's Committee. (1986). 'Black and Ethnic Minority Women.' *The Greater London Council Women's Committee Bulletin* (March): 27.
Twine, France Winddance. (2004). 'A white side of Black Britain: The concept of racial literacy.' Ethnic and Racial Studies 27(6): 878–907. https://www.tandfonline.com/doi/abs/10.1080/0141987042000268512.
Twine, France Winddance. (2010). *A White Side of Black Britain: Interracial Intimacy and Racial Literacy*. Durham and London: Duke University Press.
Walcott, Rianna. (2020). 'How the mental health system fails Black people.' Wellcome Collection. Last modified 28 January, https://wellcomecollection.org/articles/XhiLihAAACYAR42P. Accessed 29 January 2020.
Warner, Kristen J. (2017). 'In the time of plastic representation.' *Film Quarterly* Winter 2017, 71(2). Last modified 4 December, https://filmquarterly.org/2017/12/04/in-the-time-of-plastic-representation. Accessed 20 March 2020.
Watkins, S. Craig, Lombana-Bermudez, Andres, Cho, Alexander, Vickery, Jacqueline Ryan, Shaw, Vivian & Weinzimmer, Lauren. (2018). *The Digital Edge: How Black and Latino Youth Navigate Digital Inequality*. New York: New York University Press.
Wells, Jaleesa Renee & Valencia, Marta Bernal. (2017). 'Mapping the landscape of creative industries research in Scotland [software].' Edinburgh: Creative Scotland.
White, Joy. (2019). 'Growing up in "The Ends": Identity, place and belonging in an urban East London neighbourhood.' In *Identities, Youth and Belonging: International Perspectives*, edited by Sadia Habib and Michael R.M. Ward, pp. 17–33. Cham: Palgrave Macmillan.
Wilkes, Karen. (2016). *Whiteness, Weddings, and Tourism in the Caribbean: Paradise for Sale*. Basingstoke: Palgrave Macmillan.
Wilson, Melba. (1982). 'Black women writers.' Spare Rib, Issue 1982(119): 31–32.
Young, Lola. (2000). 'What is Black British feminism?' Women: A Cultural Review 11(1–2): 45–60. https://doi.org/10.1080/09574040050051415.

Open Access This chapter is licensed under the terms of the Creative Commons Attribution 4.0 International License (http://creativecommons.org/licenses/by/4.0/), which permits use, sharing, adaptation, distribution and reproduction in any medium or format, as long as you give appropriate credit to the original author(s) and the source, provide a link to the Creative Commons license and indicate if changes were made.

The images or other third party material in this chapter are included in the chapter's Creative Commons license, unless indicated otherwise in a credit line to the material. If material is not included in the chapter's Creative Commons license and your intended use is not permitted by statutory regulation or exceeds the permitted use, you will need to obtain permission directly from the copyright holder.

CHAPTER 3

Black Women's Digital, Creative, and Cultural Industry Experiences

Abstract This chapter focuses on Black women's contemporary digital, creative, and cultural industry experiences. It reflects on the overlap between tacit issues concerning racial, gender, and cultural identity in online spaces, and tensions between the emancipatory, enterprising, enjoyable and extractive dimensions of the digital experiences of Black women in Britain—which are inevitably impacted by capitalist infrastructures. This chapter addresses how labour is (un)defined and understood in society, in ways influenced by social hierarchies and structural exploitation linked to anti-Black racism, sexism, classism and different interlocking oppressions. Traumatic aspects of Black women's digital experiences are discussed, as well as the endeavours of self-serving and institutionally racist arts organisations that attempt to 'diversify' their brand image by spectacularising Black people.

Keywords Arts · Black Women · Creative · Cultural industries · Digital · Work

> ...people are just making their own spaces...it's very DIY...Making our own iconography and making our own content...it's really important that we carve out our own narratives and that we don't shy away from creating spaces for ourselves. (Ruby)

Creativity encompasses different types of communication, interactions, artistic practice, spontaneity, geographies, self-taught craft, learnt skills, making, showcasing, self-expression, documenting, storytelling, deconstructing, producing, writing, curating, collaborating, and creating. The creative work of Black women in Britain has a rich history and exists both within and outside of formal creative and cultural industry organisations (Benjamin 1995; Jones 2019; Maxwell 2018; Rae 2020; Sulter 1985; Sulter and Pollard 1990; Tajudeen and Silveira 2018; Thompson 2017; Uzor 2019). Furthermore, as is reflected on by the Spare Rib Collective (1988, p. 10), Black women's creativity can be, at once, supported and constrained by arts institutions, which are often hostile towards Black people:

> For those that take on formal art education, the experience of being isolated within the institution is demoralising. There are only a few galleries that are committed to showing Black art. Mainstream galleries have until recently remained closed to work by Black artists. When they do show our work it is often the tokenistic gesture of their equal opportunities policy. Additionally the audiences these venues court and attract is limited to the white middle class. For those Black artists that seek to intervene in that arena and to challenge the system's view of 'us', 'them' and history, there is a consistent battle against the marginalisation of our ideas as well as our practice.

As part of such writing in a 1988 issue of Spare Rib, it is asserted that a 'lack of published material on the history of Black art in this country causes problems which can only be remedied when lengthy research is carried out and published' (p. 10). More recently, Briana Pegado (2018), Founder and Director of the Edinburgh Student Arts Festival (ESAF), has critiqued inequalities in the creative and cultural industries—asking: 'if the industry does not reflect the reality of human experience, how can it be relevant?'.

To this day, Black women face institutional barriers that prohibit their access to and career progression within certain arts environments. Digital space and 'technology's overall elasticity and unpredictability' (Everett 2009, p. 12) is not free from gatekeeping and structural oppression, yet, in some cases, can offer more autonomous creative and media production opportunities for Black women than those that are available to them in many mainstream and offline contexts (Barner and Frangine 2020; Gabriel 2016; Gray 2015; Sobande 2017). This chapter emphasises 'how digital environments can simultaneously aid and limit potentially oppositional media practices; stressing the restricted nature of online experiences that may be regarded as liberating' (Sobande et al. 2019, p. 10). In this context, commercial culture is understood as encompassing 'complex dynamics between capitalism, popular culture, and today's networked media ecosystem' (Jenkins et al. 2016, pp. viii–ix).

Although not everything that people do on the internet is a form of labour (Hesmondhalgh 2010), the production and sharing of digital content by people on social media can play a central role in types of digital creative work (Abidin 2018; Glatt and Banet-Weiser, forthcoming 2021; Jarrett 2016; Jarmon 2013). What politics and power relations shape how digital content creators are identified, credited, or dismissed as digital creatives and workers? Whose creative digital work, knowledge-sharing, and cultural production is scarcely regarded as being that? How do the digital experiences of Black women involve forms of creativity and creative work? In what ways are the lives of Black people in Britain spectacularised as a result of how institutions (mis)use depictions of them? The following sections are steered by such questions as part of discussion of 'tensions between the countercultural, communal and commercial qualities of Black women's online experiences' (Sobande et al. 2019, p. 1).

(Un)defining Work, Labour, and the Marketplace

What is societally identified as a form of work and labour is influenced by social hierarchies and structural exploitation linked to racism, sexism, classism and different types of interlocking discrimination. So, when considering the work and labour experiences of Black women it is important to understand the intersectional nature of oppression (Crenshaw 1989, 2017)—such as entwined issues concerning 'inequality, relationality, power, social context, complexity, and social justice' (Hill Collins and Bilge 2016, p. 25).

To some, 'work' and 'labour' are words that capture activities and forms of productivity which clearly result in financial profit. Such capitalist-oriented perspectives can involve an emphasis on the perceived economic value of work and labour, often at the expense of any concern about the work and labour conditions that people must deal with. Throughout history and contemporary society there are many examples of Black people not entering marketplace environments out of choice, but instead being violently 'sold as a type of commodity, a labor tool, or "beast of burden"' (Henderson et al. 2016, p. 4). In the words of writers, educators, activists, and scholars Beverley Bryan et al. (2018, p. 17):

> The Black woman's experience of work in Britain mirrors our experience of work over the past five centuries. This has been one long tradition of back-breaking labour in the service of European capitalism.

The terms 'work' and 'labour' are used in this chapter to capture various activities, interactions, output, and exchanges that involve Black women producing and providing for others. This explanation of work and labour is undoubtedly ambiguous and imperfect, aligned with my intention to avoid applying narrow and prescriptive definitions that diminish the significance of everyday examples of Black women's work and labour.

My perspective of work and labour is shaped by the crucial writing of Beverley Bryan et al. (1985, 2018) on Black women's experiences of work in Britain. I am also inspired by Black feminist activists, authors, and scholars such as bell hooks (2000, p. 48) on 'women at work', as well as Angela Y. Davis (1981) whose writing about women's domestic and care work is vital. My understanding of work and labour is also guided by the writing of Black feminist activist, psychosocial studies scholar, and psychotherapist Gail Lewis (1993) regarding 'Black Women's Employment and the British Economy'—which stresses that Black women are among those who typically bear the brunt of the impact of economic crises. As hooks (2000, p. 48) states:

> When reformist feminist thinkers from privileged class backgrounds whose primary agenda was achieving social equality with men of their class equated work with liberation they meant high-paying careers. Their vision of work had little relevance for masses of women.

When reflecting on the lives of Black women in Britain in the early 1960s, Bryan et al. (2018) observe that 'the State was still busy trying to encourage (white) women to stay home and embrace domestication and consumerism. It wasn't prepared to offer any childcare support to Black women who had to work' (p. 29). Put briefly, work and labour—particularly when undertaken by Black women—does not always involve a salary, rights, or form of financial compensation or formal recognition. From strike action and the withdrawal of labour, to resistant acts at work, women continue to campaign and participate in collective action intended to challenge the many structural work and labour inequalities that impede their lives (Olufemi 2019, 2020).

Too often, notions of work and labour have been solely linked to the experiences of people in salaried roles and 'legally binding' employment contracts. To exclusively equate work and labour with individuals and institutions that are part of a paid workforce is to overlook a broad spectrum of work and labour, especially in relation to the work and labour of individuals who are among the most societally oppressed and not deemed to be British citizens. Further still, when reflecting on the digital encounters of Black women and forms of work and labour that they can involve, it is important to account for how work and labour experiences have changed in recent decades. In 2000, hooks wrote the following (p. 50):

> When women in the home spend all their time attending to the needs of others, home is a workplace for her, not a site of relaxation, comfort, and pleasure. Work outside the home has been most liberating for women who are single (many of whom live alone; they may or may not be heterosexual). Most women have not even been able to find satisfying work, and their participation in the workforce has diminished the quality of their life at home.

When considering the rise of freelance work, the digital gig economy and being remotely employed—especially amid 'lockdowns' during the COVID-19 (coronavirus) global pandemic (Sobande 2020a, b)—it is apparent that while Black women's work at home can involve attending to many other people, sometimes this involves attending to those who are not physically present in their home—such as employers and online audiences. The boundaries between working inside and outside of the home are often muddied and digitally mediated—including for Black women who work remotely and who, on some occasions, may find that working inside the home, but for an external employer, is more beneficial to them than working elsewhere. In addition, as the research of womanist theology, philosophy, and culture scholar Gabriella Beckles-Raymond (2019) indicates, for Black women in Britain, the home can be both 'a site of freedom and resistance' (p. 91).

When attempting to rethink 'the meaning of work' (hooks 2000, p. 53) it is imperative to understand the digital experiences of Black women. Although such experiences are not inherently a form of work, they often involve elements of it, especially due to consumer culture's continually 'evaporating distinctions between work and leisure, production and consumption' (Gill and Pratt 2008, p. 17). As understandings of work and labour are inextricably linked to those of the marketplace, when considering the digital work and labour experiences of Black women in Britain it is necessary to grapple with the racist and colonialist history of the development of marketplace and economic activities (Francois 2019; Grier et al. 2019; Johnson et al. 2019). Hence, this chapter is based on an awareness of 'how race functions in structural and agential ways, integrally reproducing raced markets and social conditions' (Tilly and Shilliam 2018, p. 534), which are also always connected to gendered and capitalist dynamics.

Digital Developments, Media, and the Creative and Cultural Industries

In recent years, many media brands once known for print publications and online writing decided to divest from such output and 'pivot to video'—allegedly to keep up with the changing nature of content production, saturated markets, and insatiable consumer demand. Digital developments and changes to the creative and cultural industries include those related to 'visual social media cultures' (Leaver et al. 2020) and the different ways that media is produced, shared, and monetised with the use of social media and online content-sharing platforms. Digital content-creation processes play a central role in the daily routine of many people in Britain, and blurred boundaries between production and consumption have confronted previously more fixed and dualistic notions of what determines creative work and audience engagement.

Many people's daily lives involve them concurrently producing and consuming or producing and using media content, resulting in 'prosumption' and 'produsage' (Jenkins 2006; Lind 2015). Such enmeshed processes are the bedrock of the rise of user-generated content, digital remix culture, social influencers, and micro-celebrities who create profitable digital media and brands based on their own lives and consumption habits (Abidin 2018; Abidin and Brown 2018). The 'humour infused in much digitally remixed content can initially make it seem harmless, to some' (Sobande 2019a, p. 153) but the capacity for content including memes, GIFs, and connected commentaries 'to be perceived as trivial contributes to the potency of forms of digital remix culture, which may contain hate-filled messages barely masked by allegedly comedic undertones' (ibid.).

As media and marketplace institutions are bolstered by the intersections of ableism, sexism, racism, capitalism, heteronormativity and other types of interlocking structural oppression, the digital experiences of Black women in Britain are inescapably impacted by unequal power dynamics (Akiwowo 2018; Allman 2019; Okafor 2019). Despite this, whether it is using the internet to learn about Black history that schools do not teach about (Akpan 2018; Folorunso 2018), or using it to create and share other types of knowledge so that it is accessible to many people, Black women in Britain are creatively using digital tools in ways that involve cultural production.

Studies of 'the politics of cultural and creative work' (Banks 2007) include research that illustrates the pervasiveness of institutional racism and the inadequacy of superficial so-called diversity initiatives which fail to address systemic oppression (Saha 2018)—from entry-level positions to senior management levels. As cultural theorist Angela McRobbie (2016) outlines in *Be Creative: Making a Living in the New Culture Industries*, individuals who pursue work in the creative and cultural industries can find themselves navigating many inequalities that are deeply embedded. Moreover, extensive research on the creative and cultural industries in Britain and the demographic of those who work in industry roles has 'pointed to the preponderance of youthful, able-bodied people in these fields, marked gender inequalities, high levels of educational achievement, complex entanglements of class, nationality and ethnicity, and to the relative lack of caring responsibilities undertaken by people involved in this kind of creative work' (Gill and Pratt 2008, p. 14).

'Who has the resources to live a creative life? Is an economic logic imposed in which creativity must serve a market? Who has access to the material to create?' (Roberts and Emden 2019, p. 121). Copious evidence indicates that inequalities are rife in the creative industries (Brook et al. 2018) and that '[t]he cultural economy systematically excludes people based on race, gender, class and other ascriptive qualities' (De Beukelaer and Spence 2019, p. 15). Those most impacted by associated structural disparities may attempt to circumvent some of them by primarily seeking out self-employed work in an effort to retain a certain amount of control over the environment that they work in and who they work for.

The cultural entrepreneurship research of scholars Naudin and Patel (2019) highlights how 'online platforms are an important space for self-employed cultural workers and that within this context ideas of femininity and entrepreneurship are entangled' (p. 511). Specifically focusing on the digital experiences of Black women, my research includes consideration of the encounters of those who are self-employed cultural workers. There is discussion of how the experiences of Black women online—including their entrepreneurial ones—are impacted by connected issues concerning anti-Blackness, sexism, and misogyny— specifically, misogynoir (Bailey 2010; Bailey and Trudy 2018).

Aspects of the creative and cultural industries have been identified as being 'agents of economic, social and cultural change' (Hesmondhalgh 2012, p. 8), and contemporary 'creative and cultural industries are part of what is commonly referred to as the service and knowledge economy' (Gill and Pratt 2008, p. 2). In this chapter, I identify the digital creativity and cultural production of Black women in Britain as contributing to such industry activity and innovative forms of knowledge-production and knowledge-sharing—which exceed the boundaries of digital spaces.

CARVING OUT (Y)OUR OWN SPACES AND NARRATIVES

Whether it be in the form of making newsletters, producing pamphlets, or establishing independent publishing houses, Black women in Britain have found and created routes that enable them to communicate their perspectives, creativity, politics, and work, in relatively autonomous ways. Regardless of it often being overlooked amid dominant and whitewashing discourse concerning the media in Britain, the Black press has a deep history (t)here—including the development of publications such as the *Voice*, *West Indian World*, *Black Beat International*, *Pride Magazine*, the *Caribbean Times* and the *West Indian Gazette* which was 'launched by political activist Claudia Jones a year after Ghana gained its independence' (Benjamin 1995, p. 3).

From the trailblazing work of Margaret Busby who co-founded the publishing house Allison & Busby with Clive Allison, to current digital examples of 'do it yourself (DIY)' and 'do it together (DIT)' publishing, Black women in Britain have generated new ways and spaces through which to share their views, writing, campaigning, and creative work. During the last decade, numerous media-related groups, organisations, and activities founded and predominantly led by Black women in Britain have developed. These include, but are not limited to, the non-profit *Media Diversified*, founded in 2013 by Samantha Asumadu—which tackles the under-representation and mis-representation of Black people and people of colour in the media. There has also been the creation of *Black Ballad*, a UK based lifestyle subscription membership platform that focuses on the experiences of Black British women, launched in 2014 by Tobi Oredein and her co-founder Bola Awoniyi. In addition, in 2015 Liv Little founded *gal-dem*—an online and print magazine produced by women of colour and non-binary people of colour.

The internet is home to numerous types of aesthetic-political space—created and sustained by Black women in Britain. Analogue and material media production processes such as zine-making also continue to contribute to how Black women in Britain depict themselves, record their own narratives, and participate in consciousness-raising efforts, but, sometimes, digital media still supports such offline activities—including digital marketing and archiving efforts. Digital writing and content-creation processes play a distinct role in the contemporary media experiences of many Black women in Britain, even as media producers who develop their own outlets. On the whole, the creative and cultural work of Black women in Britain is capacious—it can be found in the content of Twitter posts (Dash 2018), blogs (Gabriel 2016), and vlogs (Sobande 2017), as well as being expressed in many different ways, being embodied, and taking the form of what may be referred to as living archives (Larasi 2019).

NAVIGATING DIFFERENT DIGITAL EXPERIENCES AND THE PROSPECT OF CORPORATE CO-OPTATION

The remaining sections of this chapter are predominantly based on the words of two women who I interviewed—Bobino and Ruby. There is consideration of connections between their experiences and those of Black women creatives and artists throughout history. The comments of many who I spoke to, including Bobino and Ruby, echo those of social worker, feminist writer, public speaker, and community activist Feminista Jones (2019) who writes about the capacity for online platforms to be used to 'amplify the narratives that often go ignored by the mainstream media, which usually center Whiteness and White experiences' (p. 4). An illustration of this perspective can be found in the words of Bobino, who is an artist and researcher in her thirties and lives in England.

When interviewed, Bobino said the following about the video-sharing platform YouTube:

> I use it all the time. It's fantastic…I mean, there's the personal taken out of it, right? I don't engage with it, I don't comment on it or anything like that but I consume, and I'm constantly watching Black women from all different parts of the world. I get strength from this content…strength to expand understandings of how we can communicate…I explore, mostly.

Bobino's remarks reflect how Black women's use of social media can aid types of creativity and feelings of collectivity that contribute to the formation and visibility of an 'online Black public sphere' (Steele 2016a, p. 2). Such a perspective was expressed by most of the women who I interviewed—with the exception of Amoke who did not use social media very much—but, such discussions also involved an emphasis on the grief, harassment, and abuse that can be a part of the online visibility of Black women—especially dark-skinned Black women, who due to misogynoir (Bailey 2010; Bailey and Trudy 2018) and colourism (Adegoke 2019; Amoah 2019; Gabriel 2007; Tate 2009, 2017a, b) are frequently targeted online.

Although Twitter sometimes plays a central role in the type of collective and communal digital activity that individuals such as Bobino mentioned, it is far from being crucial to the digital experiences of all Black women in Britain. This is indicated by the view of Dr Diddly Doo who is in her thirties and based in England:

> I think that social media is a tool…and I don't know how to use the tools all the time…Twitter is one that I don't get [laughs]…I think it just doesn't naturally work with my personality. I feel that Facebook for me…it's like the original social media platform, I guess…although I would say that was Xanga, for me. Yes! [laughs] Yeah it was Xanga and then Myspace and then all the other ones started to come along. It was like Live-Journal and Tumblr and things that all came along…microblogging…at this point in my life they're more tools really…than when I was younger, like in my early twenties, it was like *life*!…it felt like everything was on there and then some quite important life lessons happened and then that changed a lot of the ways that my friends used it and I used it.

Among the Black women in Britain who I interviewed as part of my research were several who had significant experience of working in the media and creative and cultural industries, including in self-employed creative entrepreneurial roles. One of them was Ruby, who is in her twenties and based in England. Ruby spoke about learning of the flippant ways that some white people in the media industry in Britain simply suggest that writers just 'YouTube it' when trying to learn and produce allegedly 'authentic' media content about the experiences of people with different racial, ethnic, cultural, and class backgrounds to theirs.

Ruby reflected on the pervasiveness of structurally white and racist workplace cultures in the media industry, where the expertise, creativity, and talent of Black women is often overlooked and actively undermined. She commented on the challenges that Black women in Britain face when pursuing a career in the media and discussed their 'DIY' digital media culture and creation of platforms:

> There's a need to have [Black] people on the ground doing things. I'm seeing lots of Black men doing incredible things in film...there are lots of things happening...it feels like a movement...like things are finally moving, but for women it is really slow. For content creators I feel like because things are really slow...I just think it's very 'DIY'. Like, I hate the term 'millennial' but I think we're in this time when we don't want to wait anymore. We don't want to have to wait for Lenny Henry to be like, 'we need to hire more Black people' [laughs] like, people are just making their own spaces...it's very DIY...with our iPhones. Making our own iconography and making our own content...it's really important that we carve out our own narratives and that we don't shy away from creating spaces for ourselves.

Ruby's comments about the capacity for Black women in Britain to use digital technology in creative and agential ways are consistent with the findings of communication, gender, and women's studies scholar Kishonna L. Gray (2015), whose innovative research and writing illuminates how 'Black women have varied responses when employing Internet technologies for empowerment' (p. 175). Gray's (2015) detailed analysis of how recent 'communication technologies have expanded the opportunities and potential for marginalized communities to mobilize in this context counter to the dominant, mainstream media' (p. 175), is central to my understanding of many of the digital experiences that the women who I interviewed spoke of.

When discussing Black 'DIY' digital culture in Britain, Ruby recognised that due to anti-Blackness, Black men can struggle in the media industry, but that it is the interlocking impact of anti-Black racism, sexism, and misogyny (Crenshaw 1989, 2017)—more specifically, misogynoir (Bailey 2010; Bailey and Trudy 2018)—that results in the exactitudes of oppression faced by Black women. As the experiences of others who I spoke to indicate, online abuse that Black women deal with includes misogynistic harassment, colourism, and targeted trolling, including by Black men. Thus, contrary to how scholarship about, and, by Black women, is often positioned and siloed by academic institutions and disciplines—the media experiences and lives of Black women can never truly be grasped by merely focusing on factors solely to do with race *or* gender. The comments of many who I interviewed are evidence of how 'race matters no less in cyberspace than it does "IRL" (in real life)' (Kolko et al. 2000, p. 4), and how its enmeshment with issues of gender and sexuality influence the digital experiences of Black women in Britain; some of which involve so much unbridled harm being inflicted upon them—especially those who are dark-skinned—that some such individuals have withdrawn from social media and digital spaces.

Media generates 'meaning through the viewer's interpretation, which is always contingent on history, context' (Crockett 2008, p. 249). Who is classed as a media producer or content creator has evolved in tandem with technological advancements and the ascent of digital platforms, coupled with the increasingly affordable and accessible nature of some mobile devices with camera and video functions. 'However, access itself neither ensures power nor guarantees a shift in the dominant ideology' (Gray 2015, p. 175). Although it is often glibly claimed that nowadays anybody can be a media producer or content creator, factors such as ableism, fatphobia, racism, sexism, classism, xenophobia, Islamophobia, homophobia, transphobia, and other interlocking forms of oppression can impact whose production of media and creation of content is regarded as creative, skillful, and a form of work—and whose tends to be societally trivialised, devalued, and dismissed.

Ruby spoke about the work of Black content creators often involving 'really funny Vines[1]' or 'meme-worthy things', or 'Black Twitter or hair tutorials or makeup tutorials for darker skin-tones'. The influential digital content of Black women in Britain also includes vlogs on YouTube regarding university experiences and which may help other Black women to learn about aspects of university life when making related decisions (Croxford 2018). Ruby commented on the gradually rising profile and visibility of Black YouTubers and content creators, while critiquing the hyper-visibility of white middle-class YouTubers in Britain:

> ...when I think of YouTube and YouTubers in England, I think of white middle-class boys who all have the same accent [laughs]...like that regional area just outside of London, and the same editing style and the same [exaggerates voice and does a comical impression] 'hi guys!'.

Several women who I interviewed had no previous experience of vlogging and expressed an interest in pursuing work as a vlogger but were fearful of facing abuse, as they were acutely aware of how common it is for Black women who are visible online to be the target of relentless harassment and threats (Akiwowo 2018; Allman 2019; Okafor 2019). In the months following my interview with one woman she eventually established a presence as a vlogger with over 10,000 subscribers on YouTube. The content that she posts includes vlogs which feature business advice aimed at Black people and vlogs which specifically focus on what life is like for Black women in different parts of Britain and West Africa. Although YouTube may be used by Black women in ways that enrich them, including by enabling them to post and share entrepreneurial and educational video content of their own, it is also the site of a 'phenomenon, in which YouTubers attempt to reach young audiences by broadcasting far-right ideas in the form of news and entertainment' (Lewis 2018, p. 3). Thus, YouTube contributes to harm and hate speech directed at Black women and is a video-sharing platform that should not uncritically be celebrated.

As is illustrated by blogger, documentary producer, author, and scholar Renina Jarmon's (2013) insightful collection of essays—*Black Girls Are From the Future: Essays On: Race, Digital Creativity and Pop Culture*—Black women's digital creativity includes creative approaches to how they think through, write about, express, challenge and navigate socio-political issues online. Although Ruby indicated a hopefulness to do with the growth in Black women's digital content creation and their founding of creative and media-based spaces, she and others who I spoke to shared concerns pertaining to how 'the online contributions of Black women who represent themselves in ways that mainstream media rarely do, can lead to their digital re-embodied and resistant presence being mined for marketing inspiration, and their work being monetised without them being compensated' (Sobande et al. 2019, p. 10). Some of these issues are explored in more detail in the following section.

Spectacularisation and Superficiality

Despite the experiences of individuals referred to as being from 'Black, Asian and Minority Ethnic (BAME)[2]' backgrounds having been discussed in various creative and cultural industries studies, the experiences of Black women of African descent are still rarely the main focus of creative and cultural industries research and efforts to address structural barriers that constrain and obstruct people's creative practice and work. Ruby reflected on how high-profile media and arts institutions are starting to pay more attention to the independent media and content creation of Black women in Britain, but in ways that may be disingenuous and involve such institutions trying to 'tap into' different demographics:

> …so when we get approached by all these huge like, arts organisations, to do stuff… sometimes I feel like…are they actually doing it 'cause they really want to help us and want our voices to be heard, or are they tapping into a market or a group that they can't connect with?

The words of Ruby convey her understanding of how in the creative and cultural industries 'the emphasis on a more diverse media workforce is increasingly rationalized in neoliberal terms that stress the benefits of diversity for competition and economic growth, rather than for political, let alone ethical or moral reasons' (Saha 2018, p. 88).

As digital 'commerce platforms may be forging hidden ecologies and economies of inequality' (Gregory 2017, p. 5), I am aware that many forms of exploitation and oppression lurk beneath the surface of digital spaces, even those that promise to prioritise liberatory goals over profit. Ruby's comments and those of others who were interviewed about their media and digital experiences as Black women in Britain suggest that online environments 'can be a source of Black women's resistance, as well as leaving their digital commentary exposed to corporate co-optation' (Sobande et al. 2019, p. 2) and types of commodification which contrast with the intentions of the original content creator(s).

Black people around the world use digital technology and social media in ways that involve connecting and communicating with each other and communities that they are a part of (Brock 2020; Clark 2014; Everett 2009; McIlwain 2020; Mohammed 2019; Nyabola 2018; Steele 2016a, b, 2017). Resulting digital discourse is sometimes susceptible to being (re)packaged in ways that serve others' commercial interests and may even endanger the lives of those behind the original content that becomes (re)presented by others. While the commerce-driven nature of a lot of contemporary digital experiences is linked to oppressive relations and power dynamics, it is still imperative to note that 'all was not ideal in the pre-commercialization explosion of the Web' (Roberts 2019, p. 10).

It is also important to acknowledge 'different understandings of the intentions of digital content creators, some of whom produce work that is collectively owned or created to be shared in ways that move beyond notions of ownership and property which are steeped in capitalist and colonialist legacies' (Sobande 2020b). A concern expressed by some who I interviewed was that public discussions that they have on social media may be used and mined by non-Black individuals and institutions in search of material for article pitches and content that connects to Black cultural references, but without involving or crediting Black people—especially Black women (Imhotep 2019). Put another way, non-Black individuals and institutions that (mis)use signifiers of Blackness and the digital commentaries of Black people—including when attempting to pass them off as their own—may seek to use 'blackness only as a suggestion' (Jackson 2019, p. 6); alluding to a 'distance from whiteness' (Jackson 2019, p. 33) in potentially profitable ways that are aided by the fact that they themselves are *not* Black.

Keisha Williams (2018), who has studied diversity and inclusion strategies in museums, affirms that many arts and cultural industry organisations in Britain face the challenge of becoming 'recognised as an "inclusive organisation" for certain portions of the population' (p. 93) who have tended to perceive such spaces 'as not for or representing them' (ibid.). As a result, some arts and cultural organisations attempt to communicate a public image of inclusivity in ways that simply involve them drawing on superficial efforts to visually depict specific social groups as part of their self-serving marketing and communications strategies.

As curator, artist, and organiser layla-roxanne hill and I (2018, p. 109) assert when reflecting on the creative and cultural industries in Scotland:

> Not only are arts events and exhibitions located (situated somewhere, rooted in a specific and tangible space), they can also involve people – like artefacts – becoming (dis)located (moving in and out of the space in ways influenced by their access to it).

Even when Black people in Britain are excluded from creative and cultural institutions, such institutions may still attempt to imply the contrary—brazenly using images of Black people as part of their public relations approach, even without their consent and in ways that can put such people at risk of targeted abuse. When interviewed, Bobino who is in her thirties and is based in England, discussed the associated difficulties and dangers that can be involved in Black women's digital (self)representation, and how institutions (mis)use their image(s).

Bobino's words highlight how the restricted nature of the digital and creative experiences of Black women includes the risks that they are exposed to online, such as those concerning the pervasiveness of data collection in present-day society (Nzeyimana 2018), undetected surveillance, and the persistence of white supremacy which is entangled with how some individuals 'function as political influencers who adopt the techniques of brand influencers to build audiences and "sell" them on far-right ideology' (Lewis 2018, p. 1). In the words of Bobino:

> Yeah, there's the instrumentalisation that can happen…there's the cultural appropriation…there's data collection…there's…a latent or blatant narcissism. There's a spectacularisation…and superficiality…and bullying…this [social media] is not a decolonised space…it's a…it's not a safe space. I think the thing that comes into my head is that…I'm no longer on Facebook but from what I understood, these platforms can censor people speaking their truths about racism…that often…if you talk about whiteness…there seems to be algorithms that seem to shut that conversation down…I find that talking about decolonial processes, talking about racism in a language that *they* do not deem as acceptable, means that you are shutdown from having the conversation whilst racist parties and…bigoted organisations that are directly inciting violence, are allowed to…host themselves on *all* the social media platforms.

As is elucidated in the significant scholarship of sociologist Jessie Daniels (2009, 2012, 2017), white supremacy looms large within and over many digital spaces, and societies in general. Also, as the landmark work of information and communication studies scholar Safiya Umoja Noble (2018) emphasises, the internet and the creation of various algorithms is part of intersecting forms of structural oppression that negatively impact Black women in very pronounced ways. The related words of Bobino about the instrumentalisation and spectacularisation of Black people online are a reminder of how although opportunities to connect and communicate with each other can be provided by social media, these spaces are monitored, managed, and bordered in ways that can limit Black women's freedom and compromise their safety.

Many contemporary digital spaces can be understood as being impacted by 'the transition from an early nineties understanding of the Internet as a utopian space for identity play, community building, and gift economies to a more privatized, profit-driven model' (Nakamura 2008, p. 3) which favours corporate interests. While digital spaces can still be a vital source of collective-building, the potential for social media to contribute to a sense of solidarity and community is sometimes fetishised in ways that evade recognition of difficulties that can be involved in collective-building, and the importance of many physical spaces in the collective organising and lives of Black women. The creative, collective and community-oriented activities of Black women in Britain undoubtedly can, and, do, find a range of digital homes, but there is a need to also acknowledge the cost at which this sometimes comes—as well as a need to recognise that Black women's creativity, collective work, and creation of community offline is no less present or meaningful due to its lack of digital depiction or visibility.

Individuals such as Bobino spoke at length about how Black women in Britain are often structurally oppressed as part of their engagement with arts and cultural industry institutions—as both creative practitioners and audience members. In Bobino's experience, being a Black artist in Britain commonly involves navigating predominantly white spaces marked by the invisibility and hyper-visibility of Black people (Alabanza 2017). Bobino also discussed the creative work of Black women in Britain that she is thankful for and which digital and social media has played a part in:

> ...so I'm thankful that there are amazing voices on social media...from all the very many organisations like Shades of Noir and Black Blossoms and we can go on and on and on...but I just don't believe that we yet dominate the conversation and for there to be any growth, that's what needs to happen. White people need to concede the positions of power and actually hand them over. How many institutions can you name in this country that have a Black or Brown director? I've had one white woman say to me the reason that there are no Black people working at the top of these institutions is because there aren't enough Black people.

Arts organisations' claiming that 'there aren't enough Black people', in an attempt to justify the lack of Black people who work there across a range of roles, or whose creative practice is exhibited, is something that has occurred for a long time in many predominantly white places. In the introduction to *We Wanted a Revolution: Black Radical Women 1965–85: New Perspectives*—a text which accompanied a US exhibition of more than 40 artists—it is asserted that the two volumes produced in conjunction with the exhibition provide 'a direct retort to the excuse that has been offered all too frequently for these omissions in the art world: Well, we didn't know any black women artists' (Morris and Hockley 2018, p. 19). Similarities between the sentiment of these words in *We Wanted a Revolution: Black Radical Women 1965–85: New Perspectives*, and the experience Bobino shared, demonstrate the widespread and institutional nature of Black women's active exclusion from many facets of the arts, creative, and cultural industries.

As was outlined in chapter two, the idea that 'representation matters' tends to spark a range of conflicting responses and debates to do with the (in)ability of people and institutions to challenge systemic inequalities by simply pursuing increased visibility and inclusion of different social groups in public-facing contexts. Furthermore, in the words of communications and media studies scholar Akane Kanai—'conflicted feelings can be telling of where we stand and our relation to others' (2019, p. 188). The comments of Black women such as Bobino signal that certain media and cultural organisations in Britain engage in representation politics in ways that reinforce the neoliberal white supremacist foundations that they are built upon, rather than sincerely and substantially addressing structural discrimination faced by Black women and other people who are systemically oppressed.

There is an abundance of superficial forms of representation and media depiction which can obscure and distract from the hierarchical politics of the production processes and institutions behind such representations, as well as the material conditions they contribute to and emerge from. To return to the views of the Spare Rib Collective (1988, p. 9):

> Many Black artists in Britain site themselves within a Black art movement, attempting to challenge art world eurocentrism. The significant increase in the number of exhibitions by Black artists indicates that this movement has had an impact. It is encouraging to see a number of Black women artists exhibiting, organising, speaking and writing about art. However,

the dynamics of the movement and its relationship to the establishment is problematic on a number of fronts. Progress has been difficult to quantify.

These words featured in Spare Rib (1988) remain highly applicable to the creative experiences of many Black women in Britain, some of whom are making use of digital and social media as a core component of their creative practice or the ways that they share and exhibit it.

SOCIAL MEDIA TERMS OF SERVICE, SHADOWBANNING, AND SURVEILLANCE

Digital platforms and online social networking services such as Twitter are continually used as part of the development and sharing of the creative content and critical cultural writing of Black women around the world. Twitter's 140 characters or less approach to posts that people could tweet shifted with its introduction of a maximum of 280 characters in 2017. Despite the micro-blogging site's focus on concise content, it has been used by Black women in ways that involve sharing detailed and impactful writing and analysis of issues—including their thoughts on and experiences of politics and pop culture (Clark 2014; Jones 2019).

Twitter's Terms of Service (TOS) which grant Twitter a license (and the right to sublicense) which is worldwide, non-exclusive, and royalty free, are symptomatic of the relative lack of control that people have over the content that they create and share there. Such TOS are but one of many examples of the considerably restricted nature of the rights of digital content creators. Further still, Instagram's shadowbanning approach which has involved them strategically hiding content that is subjectively deemed to be 'sexually suggestive' has impacted the digital content and work of Black women (Joseph 2019).

Shadowbanning disproportionately negatively affects people whose existence, due to racism, sexism, homophobia, fatphobia, transphobia, and other types of intersecting oppressions, is often demonised and a source of moral panic in society. Shadowbanning has resulted in censoring of the digital presence and content of pole athletes and dancers (Carolina 2019), LGBTQIA+ Black women, sex workers, and plus-size models; even when there is an absence of nudity in images (Salty 2019). Due to anti-Blackness, cis-normativity, and transphobia, trans* and non-binary Black people face relentless forms of oppression, brutality, and surveillance (Alabanza 2018). The extensiveness of cis-normativity and transphobia is such that Black trans* and non-binary people face harassment, abuse, and violence from cisgender Black people as well as non-Black people who target them online and offline.

Whose physical appearance and embodiment is identified as being 'sexually suggestive' by Instagram as part of their shadowbanning approach is shaped by the different ways that certain people—including Black women, trans* and non-binary people—are more systemically policed and societally framed as hypersexualised than others. For some, the impact that shadowbanning has on the visibility of their digital content can result in a loss of income and can exacerbate precarious living conditions. How shadowbanning unfolds reveals a lot about whose lives, work, and self-representation efforts are treated as acceptable and something to celebrate, and whose are not and are subject to institutional attempts to hide, condone, and erase them.

In 2019 TikTok admitted to having suppressed the reach of videos by creators that they assume are vulnerable to cyberbullying, including disabled creators (Kim 2019). Such an approach is another example of whose presence on the internet is most likely to be constrained due to a matrix of domination (Hill Collins 2000). The examples of TikTok's suppression of content, and shadowbanning on Instagram, are just two which illustrate that although social media may be used by Black women as part of their creative and cultural work—and, even, their liberationist efforts—such experiences can involve them enduring forms of censoring that reflect their longstanding systemic oppression and surveillance.

Regardless of how some digital spaces may seem free(er) of capitalist and commercial binds than other contexts, as the internet often operates and is used 'as a trading platform' (Dy et al. 2017, p. 300), much digital activity is spawned by inherently capitalistic structures. Consequently, while Black women in Britain may find that digital spaces can facilitate their creative work, in some ways, they may also find—intentionally and otherwise—that their digital creativity contributes to types of marketing, branding, and commercial activity. Given that there is 'a whole brand of (mostly digital) journalism that culls social media content for stories' (McMillan Cottom 2017, p. 221), Black women's attempts to maintain control of digital creativity, content, and commentaries that they generate involve navigating commercial institutions' ever-present extractive gaze and hunger for profit.

Although social media is often regarded as more democratised than other older media production avenues—such as print newspapers and broadcast television—social media certainly does not exist outside of hierarchical relations. For every Black woman in Britain who may have found that social media has helped them to establish their creative and cultural practice, there may be another who feels as though they have fallen foul—including because of cliquish qualities of aspects of digital culture and the dangers that their digital visibility can involve. After all, an individual's ability to access a space does not always mean being able to participate in it in ways that are beneficial to them (Gray 2015).

Harassment, Bullying, and Abuse

As has been established, the digital experiences of Black women can bolster their creativity and resistant work (Jarmon 2013) but can also be impacted by the common ways that Black women have been 'subjected to a scrutinizing surveillance' (Browne 2015, p. 156) for centuries. As is explained by communication, gender, and women's studies scholar Kishonna L. Gray and critical culture, gender, and race studies scholar David J. Leonard (2018), in their work on *Woke Gaming: Digital Challenges to Oppression and Social Injustice* (p. 5):

> From the Internet to the constructive worlds of virtual gameplay, the digital world offers spaces of play and freedom in a post-ism promised land of equality and justice, but our experiences reveal the fissures found within those spaces.

Among the many ways that the digital encounters of Black women in Britain involve experiencing harm and harassment, is how they are objectified and spectacularised by white editors in search of content to generate sales and clicks—including in the form of Black women's potentially marketable writing about traumatic and painful experiences. Independent writer Kesiena Boom's (2019) discussion of challenges involved in producing Black women's personal feminist essays in digital spheres exposes such issues, and poignantly poses the question: 'can the price ever be right?' (p. 252). Overall, different digital spaces may enable Black women's public documentation of encountering oppression, profiling, and abuse, but can also be a source of such experiences.

As Bobino spoke about at length, when Black women in Britain are visible in media and public life, they are prime targets of hate speech and potential violence. For example, Labour Member of Parliament

(MP) Diane Abbott was subject to nearly 50% of online harassment directed at women MPs in the lead up to the British election in 2017 (Dhrodia 2018), and continues to face excessive amounts of public scrutiny rooted in misogynoir (Palmer 2019). Research also indicates that Black women are 84% more likely than white women to be mentioned in abusive Twitter comments (Amnesty International 2018). As such, there is a need for non-partisan and not-for-profit organisations including *Glitch*—founded by Seyi Akiwowo in 2017—which works towards ending abuse online and has supported and driven research about the specific experiences of Black women in Britain.

A Black cyberfeminist framework which 'argues that structural oppression is translated through technologies and reproduces different individual and categorical experiences' (McMillan Cottom 2017, p. 217) can aid understanding of the many dangers and forms of oppression that Black women encounter on the internet. And so, it is from a Black cyberfeminist perspective (Gray 2015) that I continue to consider the thoughts and experiences of individuals such as Bobino, who described some of the ways that social media can be a 'toxic place' which instead of bringing joy to the lives of Black women, can, at times, curtail their wellbeing:

> I think it might've been around 10 years ago [that I joined social media]. I didn't want to be on it. My friends said you've got to be on it, everyone's on it. It's how you keep in touch with people, but to be honest I think it's a trap. It's great for information…but I can look down my Twitter timeline for instance and see the actual…see those images of atrocity…Black people spectacularised…their death…I can't watch these videos of inhumane practices that we are continuing to carry out as a country…I can't look through my timeline and not feel complicit…so I don't really engage with Twitter anymore.

'As anti-Black racism and other forms of outright bigotry experience a click-inducing upswing in popularity' (Spelic 2019, p. 42), the digital lives of Black women in Britain, and, around the world, continue to be marred by the prospect and reality of encountering disturbing content that depicts and communicates violence. The leading information studies work of Sarah T. Roberts (2019) on the experiences of commercial content moderators emphasises how continual exposure to extremely disturbing content can have a very detrimental impact on people's lives and health. Relatedly, Bobino's words stress that the trauma which can be involved in Black women's online experiences can be connected to horrifically violent, anti-Black, and white supremacist content that they are exposed to, sometimes, daily.

Even when speaking of the negative aspects of social media, Bobino consistently acknowledged some of its benefits for Black women in Britain, including how particular platforms may lend themselves to Black women's creativity:

> I see amazing people online. I see my peers online doing amazing things…resisting…but to tell you the truth, I'm really struggling. I'm not feeling like…I don't feel that social media is necessarily boosting my self-esteem or my confidence, but then again I do see amazing people, so I shouldn't say that…maybe it's because I'm not fully present with myself or I'm giving myself a hard time, so I'm not able to celebrate with other wonderful…I think that what it is that digital spaces can do is persuade you to go and spend time with people face to face. I'm mostly using Instagram. It allows me to be creative when…it allows me to create visual work in a way, or think through things visually. I also realise that [with social media] you're able to…celebrate yourself and celebrate others…celebrate difference and experiment with new ways of representing yourself and speaking language…I mean…that is a triumph that we can do that and disseminate it and we can get feedback. We can validate ourselves but I also really, really am troubled by systems of measurement. I'm worried that person 'A' will want to replicate person 'B', and I see this again especially in terms of our media and our social media and an emphasis on brand and consumption…homogenisation.

In a similar way to Ruby, Bobino recalled her awareness of how certain media and arts organisations attempt to use images of Black women and their content and creative work in profit-oriented and shallow ways which simply serve the organisation. She also spoke of how such organisations attempt to virtue-signal by indicating their awareness of some of the abuse that Black people face, but without critically addressing this or acknowledging such experiences within their own institutions:

> They [arts organisations] are interested in spectacularising stories of abuse. They do not have the tools with which to have conversations about race, so when I brought to their [an organisation's] attention, their complicity…when we penetrate into those spheres, at the moment it's superficial, because they are not allies. They have no interest and no will to have a

conversation about their complicit racism, so what I mean about camaraderie [that organisations claim to offer] is the superficiality that runs rampant with neoliberal white supremacist patriarchal misogyny, and in fact, many of these women are misogynistic in as much as they are not willing to make the connection between race, sexism, and class. When I spoke to them about how the organisation is not representing me and my brothers and sisters, Black and brown in the UK…they said 'we've got [name of one Black woman employee]' …I say all this in relation to how they use media, as I noticed on their Instagram they'll often have an image of a Black person sat outside looking like they were minding their own business…they've instrumentalised this young Black person. I think there needs to be a whole rewriting of it…people of colour…Black women need to be making these programmes and these platforms. I think we take what we can from those [digital] platforms and what we've learnt from them and arrange it into something that is 'decolonised'.

Bobino's words emphasise that the mere inclusion of people from various backgrounds and with different identities in the creative and cultural industries does not equate to them being treated equally. The example that she discussed which involved an arts institution attempting to 'diversify' their brand image, rather than address structural racism and anti-Blackness within the institution, is demonstrative of how 'whether TV or tech, cosmetic diversity too easily stands in for substantive change, with a focus on feel good differences like food, language, and dress, not on systemic disadvantages associated with employment, education, and policing' (Benjamin 2019, pp. 19–20).

Bobino's comments also highlight how some arts organisations tokenistically engage with Black women, including by framing their hiring of just one Black woman—who is often from a middle-class background—as a revolutionary declaration of their support of Black people and Black art. Such industry dynamics are consistent with the words of the Spare Rib Collective (1988, p. 10): 'The establishment, as it does with Black communities and other interest groups, attempts to identify particular individuals as the authenticating voices…marginalised individuals alone do not represent a forceful challenge to the mainstream'. The examples that Bobino mentioned are consistent with 'an economy of visibility' (Banet-Weiser 2018, p. 2), within which (re)presentations of Black people are used by brands and institutions that attempt to position themselves as 'diverse' and 'inclusive'—words often emptied of meaning—and, even, 'radical'—despite their contrary actions.

As has been argued, 'the analysis of textual representations of race in advertising imagery is only a part of the broader project of documenting the historical relationship between race and consumption' (Lury 2001, p. 157). Bobino's comments evidence the importance of looking beyond the digitally marketed image of an arts organisation and learning about Black people's experiences of them—expressed in their own words—to understand how they are treated by such institutions.

Many brands, I argue, including in the creative and cultural industries, '(mis)use issues concerning commercialised notions of feminism, equality and Black social justice activism as part of marketing that flattens and reframes liberationist politics while upholding the neoliberal idea that achievement and social change requires individual ambition and consumption rather than structural shifts and resistance' (Sobande 2019b, p. 1). Thus, even when the activities of creative and cultural industry institutions in Britain are marketed as foregrounding matters regarding anti-Black racism, Black lives, and intersecting oppressions, it is rare that such activities meaningfully involve, engage, support, and are led by Black women—especially those from working-class backgrounds.

The experiences of Black women in Britain, particularly at regional levels, are often invisible amid data and discourse concerning issues connected to gender, race, accessibility, inclusion, and the creative and cultural industries (hill and Sobande 2018). In fact, their so-called 'statistical insignificance' is often the shoddy basis upon which some creative and cultural industry organisations claim they are not able to recruit and employ Black women, or provide specific and transparent information about the extent to which they work with Black creatives. Regardless of little to no indication of a substantial effort and commitment to address structural inequalities and support the creativity, craft, and work of Black women, many arts organisations continue to construct an image of them that suggests the opposite. However, often with the use of digital technology and social media, Black women in Britain are raising awareness of and publicly challenging such approaches.

Concluding Thoughts

As is explored in essential work which develops a Black cyberfeminism framework (Gray 2015), Black women are using digital spaces and technology as part of Black feminist knowledge-production, community building, and creative work. Creativity can be found in Black women's kinship, support of each other and amplification of their voices and experiences online, as well as their efforts to communicate and resist certain political positions and actions. Ultimately, Black women's creativity is expansive and includes Black feminist forms, as 'Black feminism is always a creative and dynamic production of thinking and living otherwise' (Emejulu and Sobande 2019, p. 3).

The words of both Ruby and Bobino are a reminder of how despite the opportunities to connect and communicate with each other that social media may provide for Black people around the world, such spaces are monitored, managed—and, arguably—bordered in ways that can considerably limit Black women's creative control, free speech, and can even compromise their safety. Whether they are participating as workers, spectators, creators or all three interconnected roles, the marketplace can be a site of Black women's sustained oppression, as well as a site of their efforts to exert agency and push against forms of structural marginalisation and brutality. For that reason, I remain wary of suggesting that liberation can be secured within marketplace settings, but also conscious of how Black women participate in such contexts in resistant ways and as part of liberationist struggles that far surpass the parameters of consumer culture (Sobande and Osei 2020).

While my work 'relates to issues of representation, it is also focused on power and politics, because without transformational and structural changes, increased surface-level representation is meaningless' (hill and Sobande 2018, p. 109), and can be institutionally weaponised to distract from prevailing societal inequalities and necessary critique of them. For decades, 'Black women's struggles for political change have led to an increased involvement in a number of fields, amongst them education, media, local government, health and the arts' (Spare Rib 1988, p. 9). Even though Black women in Britain are significantly shaping creative and cultural production (t)here, including via the creation of digital content, their work seldom receives adequate support and is often trivialised to the point that it is completely dismissed. However, it is equally important to note continually increasing commercial and corporate interest in the digital activities of Black people, as is evidenced by YouTube hosting the YouTube Black summit event in Los Angeles in 2016, and Twitter hosting a Black Twitter UK event at their London headquarters in 2019.

As is reflected on in this chapter, the digital experiences of Black women in Britain include the production and sharing of content as part of creative, and, sometimes, resistant, efforts—including activist work which involves documenting collective organising and offline action. Still, 'potentially resistant and liberating qualities of such experiences can be denuded through forms of corporate co-optation; Black women's online content being (mis)used and (mis)appropriated by commercial entities that fail to credit or consult the creator(s) of the original source' (Sobande et al. 2019, p. 11). As the digital activity of Black women is an increasing source of interest among mainstream media and marketplace institutions, digital content and narratives created by Black women will continue to be (re)mediated by commercial entities, including creative and cultural industry organisations in Britain. Therefore, some of the ways that the digital dialogue of Black women may seem to transcend certain borders—including the borders of different social media platforms and institutions—can sometimes be to their detriment and to the benefit of corporations that quickly attempt to commodify Blackness, especially the creativity, candour, and ingenuity of Black women.

Notes

1. Launched in 2013, Vine was a video hosting service where people could upload, share and respond to short-form video content that was approximately six seconds long. Although Vine is defunct (since 2016), it continues to be recognised as a key site of viral content created and shared by Black people, as is discussed in online articles such as 'Black Vine: The Oral History of a Six-Second Movement' (Félix 2016). In January 2020 Byte was released which is a short-form video hosting service that has been framed as Vine's successor.
2. The term 'BAME' which stands for Black, Asian and Minority Ethnic is one which rightly continues to be critiqued, including due to its use often involving a lack of specificity concerning racial and ethnic identities and experiences; especially at the expense of understandings of the lives of Black people of African descent and the particularities of anti-Blackness that they encounter. For this reason, the term 'BAME' only features in this book as part of discussion of prior writing and research that makes use of it in connection to the lives of Black women.

References

Abidin, Crystal. (2018). *Internet Celebrity: Understanding Fame Online*. Bingley: Emerald.
Abidin, Crystal & Brown, Megan Lindsay. (eds.) (2018). *Microcelebrity Around the Globe: Approaches to Cultures of Internet Fame*. Bingley: Emerald.

Adegoke, Yomi. (2019). 'Dark skinned women are now being celebrated, but don't blame us for scepticism.' *Metro*. Last modified 23 August, https://metro.co.uk/2019/08/23/dark-skinned-women-are-now-being-celebrated-but-dont-blame-us-for-scepticism-10619341. Accessed 5 November 2019.

Akiwowo, Seyi. (2018). 'Amnesty's latest research into online abuse finally confirms what Black women have known for over a decade.' *Huffington Post*. Last Modified 19 December, https://www.huffingtonpost.co.uk/entry/amnesty-online-abuse-women-twitter_uk_5c1a0a2fe4b02d2cae8ea0c1. Accessed 17 January 2019.

Akpan, Paula. (2018). 'Social media has taught me more about black British history than I ever learned in school—and that's a crying shame.' *The Independent*. Last modified 7 October, https://www.independent.co.uk/voices/black-history-month-social-media-nottingham-race-riots-reni-eddo-lodge-claudia-jones-martin-luther-a8572701.html. Accessed 15 June 2019.

Alabanza, Travis. (2017). *The Other'd Artist/s*. Glasgow: Transmission.

Alabanza, Travis. (2018). 'Dear Naomi: We need to say her name.' *gal-dem*. Last modified 28 March, http://gal-dem.com/silence-failing-naomi-hersi. Accessed 5 April 2018.

Allman, Esme. (2019). 'The dark side of social media for Black women.' *Black Ballad*. Last Modified 14 February, https://blackballad.co.uk/people/the-dark-side-of-social-media-for-black-women?listIds=5d93b25a88157fff350b6d2e. Accessed 20 February 2019.

Amnesty International. (2018). 'Women abused on Twitter every 30 seconds—New study.' *Amnesty International*. Last modified 18 December, https://www.amnesty.org.uk/press-releases/women-abused-twitter-every-30-seconds-new-study. Accessed 7 January 2019.

Amoah, Susuana. (2019). '#NoShade: A critical analysis of digital influencer activism against shadeism in the beauty industry.' *Academia.edu*, https://www.academia.edu/39881809/NoShade_A_Critical_Analysis_of_Digital_Influencer_Activism_Against_Shadeism_in_the_Beauty_Industry. Accessed 30 July 2019.

Bailey, Moya. (2010). 'They aren't talking about me …' *Crunk Feminist Collective*. Last modified 14 March, http://www.crunkfeministcollective.com/2010/03/14/they-arent-talking-about-me/. Accessed 28 March 2020.

Bailey, Moya & Trudy. (2018). 'On misogynoir: Citation, erasure, and plagiarism.' *Feminist Media Studies* 18(4): 762–768. https://doi.org/10.1080/14680777.2018.1447395.

Banet-Weiser, Sarah. (2018). *Empowered: Popular Feminism and Popular Misogyny*. Durham and London: Duke University Press.

Banks, Mark. (2007). *The Politics of Cultural Work*. Basingstoke: Palgrave Macmillan.

Barner, Briana & Frangine, Sacrée. (2020). 'Safe and sound: How podcasts became audio enclaves for Black women.' *Bitch Media*. Last modified 26 February, https://www.bitchmedia.org/article/podcasts-audio-enclaves-black-women. Accessed 26 February 2020.

Beckles-Raymond, Gabriella. (2019). 'Revisiting the home as a site of freedom and resistance.' In *To Exist is to Resist: Black Feminism in Europe*, edited by Akwugo Emejulu & Francesca Sobande, pp. 91–102. London: Pluto Press.

Benjamin, Ionie. (1995). *The Black Press in Britain*. Staffordshire: Trentham Books.

Benjamin, Ruha. (2019). *Race After Technology: Abolitionist Tools for the New Jim Code*. Cambridge and Medford, MA: Polity Press.

Boom, Kesiena. (2019). 'But some of us are tired: Black women's "personal feminist essays" in the digital sphere.' In *To Exist is to Resist: Black Feminism in Europe*, edited by Akwugo Emejulu & Francesca Sobande, pp. 245–258. London: Pluto Press.

Brock, André. (2020). *Distributed Blackness: African American Cybercultures*. New York: New York University Press.

Brook, Orian, O'Brien, Dave & Taylor, Mark. (2018). 'Panic! It's an arts emergency: Panic! social class, taste and inequalities in the creative industries.' *Create London*. Last modified 18 April, https://createlondon.org/wp-content/uploads/2018/04/Panic-Social-Class-Taste-and-Inequalities-in-the-Creative-Industries1.pdf. Accessed 15 May 2019.

Browne, Simone. (2015). *Dark Matters: On the Surveillance of Blackness*. Durham: Duke University Press.

Bryan, Beverley, Dadzie, Stella & Scafe, Suzanne. (1985). *The Heart of the Race: Black Women's Lives in Britain*. London: Virago.

Bryan, Beverley, Dadzie, Stella & Scafe, Suzanne. (2018). *The Heart of the Race: Black Women's Lives in Britain* (2nd ed.). London: Verso.

Carolina. (2019). 'What Instagram's pole dance shadowban means for social media.' *Blogger on Pole*. Last modified 23 July, https://bloggeronpole.com/2019/07/what-instagram-pole-dance-shadowban-means-for-social-media. Accessed 3 February 2020.

Clark, Meredith D. (2014). 'To tweet our own cause: A mixed-methods study of the online phenomenon "Black Twitter".' Chapel Hill, NC: University of North Carolina at Chapel Hill Graduate School, 2014. https://doi.org/10.17615/7bfs-rp55.

Crenshaw, Kimberlé. (1989). 'Demarginalizing the intersection of race and sex: A Black feminist critique of antidiscrimination doctrine, feminist theory and antiracist politics.' *University of Chicago Legal Forum* 1989(1): 139–167. https://chicagounbound.uchicago.edu/uclf/vol1989/iss1/8.

Crenshaw, Kimberlé. (2017). *On Intersectionality: Essential Writings*. New York: The New Press.

Crockett, David. (2008). 'Marketing blackness: How advertisers use race to sell products.' *Journal of Consumer Culture* 8(2): 245–268. https://journals.sagepub.com/doi/10.1177/1469540508090088.

Croxford, Rianna. (2018). 'What it is like for a black student to go to Cambridge.' *Financial Times*. Last modified 31 May 2018, https://www.ft.com/content/cad952d2-215d-11e8-8d6c-a1920d9e946f. Accessed 2 June 2018.

Daniels, Jessie. (2009). *Cyber Racism: White Supremacy Online and the New Attack on Civil Rights*. New York: Rowman & Littlefield.

Daniels, Jessie. (2012). 'Race and racism in Internet Studies: A review and critique.' *New Media & Society* 15(5): 695–719. https://doi.org/10.1177/1461444812462849.

Daniels, Jessie. (2017). 'Twitter and white supremacy, a love story.' *DAME Magazine*. Last modified 19 October, https://www.damemagazine.com/2017/10/19/twitter-and-white-supremacy-love-story. Accessed 10 July 2019.

Dash, Danielle. (2018). 'Guest blog: Hypervisible black women and twitter.' *Tiata Fahodzi*. Last modified 12 January, http://www.tiatafahodzi.com/blog/guest-blog-hypervisibile-black-women-twitter-danielle-dash. Accessed 17 November 2019.

Davis, Angela Y. (1981). *Women, Race & Class*. New York: Random House.

De Beukelaer, Christiaan & Spence, Kim-Marie. (2019). *Global Cultural Economy*. London: Routledge.

Dhrodia, Azmina. (2018). 'Unsocial media: A toxic place for women.' *IPPR Progressive Review* 24(4): 380–387. https://doi.org/10.1111/newe.12078.

Dy, Angela Martinez, Marlow, Susan & Martin, Lee. (2017). 'A Web of opportunity or the same old story? Women digital entrepreneurs and intersectionality theory.' *Human Relations* 70(3): 286–311. https://doi.org/10.1177/0018726716650730.

Emejulu, Akwugo & Sobande, Francesca. (eds.) (2019). *To Exist is to Resist: Black Feminism in Europe*. London: Pluto Press.

Everett, Anna. (2009). *Digital Diaspora: A Race for Cyberspace*. Albany, NY: SUNY Press.

Félix, Doreen St. (2016). 'Black vine: The oral history of a six-second movement.' *MTV*. Last modified 4 November, http://www.mtv.com/news/2951355/black-vine-oral-history. Accessed 17 June 2018.

Folorunso, Tomiwa. (2018). 'Learning about Black Scottish history! [video].' *BBC the Social*. Last modified 23 October, https://www.bbc.co.uk/programmes/p06pnf2y. Accessed 9 June 2019.

Francois, Janine. (2019). 'The future of climate activism must centre people of colour.' *The Huffington Post*. Last modified 3 May 2019, https://www.huf

fingtonpost.co.uk/entry/climate-change-people-of-colour_uk_5cc96b37e4b0 076cfb2a8a0a. Accessed 7 January 2020.

Gabriel, Deborah. (2007). *Layers of Blackness: Colourism in the African Diaspora.* London: Imani Media Ltd.

Gabriel, Deborah. (2016). 'Blogging while Black, British and female: A critical study on discursive activism.' *Information, Communication & Society* 19(11): 1622–1635. https://doi.org/10.1080/1369118X.2016.1146784.

Gill, Rosalind & Pratt, Andy. (2008). 'In the social factory?: Immaterial labour, precariousness and cultural work.' *Theory, Culture & Society* 25(7–8): 1–30. https://journals.sagepub.com/doi/10.1177/0263276408097794.

Glatt, Zoë & Banet-Weiser, Sarah. (forthcoming, 2021). 'Productive ambivalence, economies of visibility and the political potential of feminist YouTubers.' In *Creator Culture: Studying the Social Media Entertainment Industry*, edited by Stuart Cunningham & David Craig. New York, NY: New York University Press.

Gray, Kishonna L. (2015). 'Race, gender, and virtual inequality: Exploring the liberatory potential of Black cyberfeminist theory.' In *Produsing Theory in a Digital World 2.0: The Intersection of Audiences and Production in Contemporary Theory*, Vol. 2, edited by Rebecca Ann Lind, pp. 175–192. New York: Peter Lang.

Gray, Kishonna L. & Leonard, David J. (eds.) (2018). *Woke Gaming: Digital Challenges to Oppression and Social Injustice.* Seattle: University of Washington Press.

Gregory, Karen. (2017). 'Structure and agency in a digital world.' In *Digital Sociologies*, edited by Jessie Daniels, Karen Gregory & Tressie McMillan Cottom, pp. 3–7. Bristol and Chicago: Policy Press.

Grier, Sonya A., Thomas, Kevin D. & Johnson, Guillaume D. (2019). 'Re-imagining the marketplace: Addressing race in academic marketing research.' *Consumption, Markets & Culture* 22(1): 91–100. https://doi.org/10.1080/10253866.2017.1413800.

Henderson, Geraldine Rosa, Hakstian, Anne-Marie & Williams, Jerome D. (eds.) (2016). *Consumer Equality: Race and the American Marketplace (Racism in American Institutions).* Santa Barbara: Praeger.

Hesmondhalgh, David. (2010). 'User-generated content, free labour and the cultural industries.' *Ephemera: Theory and Politics in Organization* 10(3/4): 267–284.

Hesmondhalgh, David. (2012). *The Cultural Industries* (3rd ed.). London: Sage.

hill, layla-roxanne & Sobande, Francesca. (2018). 'In our own words: organising and experiencing exhibitions as Black women and women of colour in Scotland.' In *Accessibility, Inclusion, and Diversity in Critical Event Studies*, edited by Rebecca Finkel, Briony Sharp & Majella Sweeney, pp. 107–121. New York: Routledge.

Hill Collins, Patricia. (2000). *Black Feminist Thought: Knowledge, Consciousness, and the Politics of Empowerment* (2nd ed.). New York and London: Routledge.
Hill Collins, Patricia & Bilge, Sirma. (2016). *Intersectionality*. Cambridge: Polity Press.
hooks, bell. (2000). *Feminism is for Everybody: Passionate Politics*. London and New York: Routledge.
Imhotep, Malika. (2019). '#OnFleek: Authorship, interpellation, and the Black femme prowess of Black Twitter.' In *#Identity: Hashtagging Race, Gender, Sexuality, and Nation*, edited by Abigail De Kosnik and Keith P. Feldman, pp. 39–56. Ann Arbor: University of Michigan Press.
Jackson, Lauren Michele. (2019). *White Negroes: When Cornrows Were in Vogue… and Other Thoughts on Cultural Appropriation*. Boston: Beacon Press.
Jarmon, Renina (@ReninaJarmon). (2013). *Black Girls Are From the Future: Essays On: Race, Digital Creativity and Pop Culture*. Washington, DC: Jarmon Media.
Jarrett, Kylie. (2016). *Feminism, Labour and Digital Media: The Digital Housewife*. New York: Routledge.
Jenkins, Henry. (2006). *Convergence Culture: Where Old and New Media Collide*. New York: New York University Press.
Jenkins, Henry, Ito, Mizuko & boyd, danah. (2016). *Participatory Culture in a Networked Era: A Conversation on Youth, Learning, Commerce, and Politics*. Cambridge and Malden, MA: Polity Press.
Johnson, Guillaume D., Thomas, Kevin. D., Harrison, Anthony K. & Grier, Sonya A. (2019). *Race in the Marketplace: Crossing Critical Boundaries*. Cham: Palgrave Macmillan.
Jones, Dorett. (2019). 'Through our lens: Filming our resistance. Does the future look Black in Europe?' In *To Exist is to Resist: Black Feminism in Europe*, edited by Akwugo Emejulu & Francesca Sobande, pp. 273–283. London: Pluto Press.
Jones, Feminista. (2019). *Reclaiming Our Space: How Black Feminists Are Changing the World from the Tweets to the Streets*. Boston: Beacon Press.
Joseph, Chanté. (2019). 'Instagram's murky 'shadow bans' just serve to censor marginalised communities.' *The Guardian*. Last modified 8 November, https://www.theguardian.com/commentisfree/2019/nov/08/instagram-shadow-bans-marginalised-communities-queer-plus-sized-bodies-sexually-suggestive. Accessed 7 January 2020.
Kanai, Akane. (2019). *Gender and Relatability in Digital Culture: Managing Affect, Intimacy and Value*. Cham: Palgrave Macmillan.
Kim, Michelle. (2019). 'TikTok admits it suppressed reach of queer, fat, and disabled creators.' *Them*. Last modified 6 December, https://www.them.us/

story/tiktok-suppressed-fat-queer-disabled-creators. Accessed 15 December, 2019.

Kolko, Beth E., Nakamura, Lisa & Rodman, Gilbert B. (eds.) (2000). *Race in Cyberspace*. New York and London: Routledge.

Larasi, Marai. (2019). 'Foreword.' In *This Is Us: Black British Women and Girls*, curated by Kafayat Okanlawon, pp. 5–9. London: Break the Habit Press.

Leaver, Tama, Highfield, Tim & Abidin, Crystal. (2020). *Instagram: Visual Social Media Cultures*. Cambridge: Polity Press.

Lewis, Gail. (1993). 'Black women's employment and the British economy.' In *Inside Babylon: The Caribbean Diaspora in Britain*, edited by Winston James & Clive Harris, pp. 73–96. London: Verso.

Lewis, Rebecca. (2018), 'Alternative influence: Broadcasting the reactionary right on YouTube.' *Data & Society*. https://datasociety.net/wp-content/uploads/2018/09/DS_Alternative_Influence.pdf. Accessed 15 March 2019.

Lind, Rebecca Ann. (ed.) (2015). *Produsing Theory in a Digital World 2.0: The Intersection of Audiences and Production in Contemporary Theory*, Vol. 2, New York: Peter Lang.

Lury, Celia. (2001). *Consumer Culture*. Cambridge: Polity Press.

Maxwell, Hailey. (2018). 'Exploring art's class problem.' *Conter*. Last modified 10 May, https://www.conter.co.uk/blog/2018/5/10/exploring-arts-class-problem. Accessed 15 May 2018.

McIlwain, Charlton. D. (2020). *Black Software: The Internet and Racial Justice, from the AfroNet to Black Lives Matter*. New York: Oxford University Press.

McMillan Cottom, Tressie. (2017). 'Black cyberfeminism: Ways forward for intersectionality and digital sociology.' In *Digital Sociologies*, edited by Jessie Daniels, Karen Gregory & Tressie McMillan Cottom, pp. 211–231. Bristol and Chicago: Policy Press.

McRobbie, Angela. (2016). *Be Creative: Making a Living in the New Cultural Industries*. Cambridge and Malden, MA: Polity Press.

Mohammed, Wunpini Fatimata. (2019). 'Online activism: Centering marginalized voices in activist work.' *Ada: A Journal of Gender, New Media & Technology* 15. https://adanewmedia.org/2019/02/issue15-mohammed.

Morris, Catherine & Hockley, Rujeko. (2018). *We Wanted a Revolution: Black Radical Women 1965–85*. Brooklyn Museum, Distributed by Duke University Press.

Nakamura, Lisa. (2008). *Digitizing Race: Visual Cultures of the Internet*. Minneapolis: University of Minnesota Press.

Naudin, Annette & Patel, Karen. (2019). 'Entangled expertise: Women's use of social media in entrepreneurial work.' *European Journal of Cultural Studies* 22(5–6): 511–527. https://doi.org/10.1177/1367549417743037.

Noble, Safiya Umoja. (2018). *Algorithms of Oppression: How Search Engines Reinforce Racism*. New York: New York University Press.

Nyabola, Nanjala. (2018). *Digital Democracy, Analogue Politics: How the Internet Era Is Transforming Politics in Kenya*. London: Zed Books.

Nzeyimana, Natalie. (2018). 'Clicks for kicks: how we came to trade our private data for joy.' *Prospect*. Last modified 20 December, https://www.prospectmagazine.co.uk/politics/data-security-facebook-how-we-came-to-trade-our-private-data-for-joy. Accessed 19 November 2019.

Okafor, Kelechi. (2019). 'Clemmie Hooper is a midwife—That's why her trolling really matters.' Last modified 12 November, https://graziadaily.co.uk/life/real-life/clemmie-hooper-trolling-midwife. Accessed 17 January 2020.

Olufemi, Lola. (2019). 'Women: Stop working!' *New Internationalist*. Last modified 7 March, https://newint.org/features/2019/03/07/women-stop-working. Accessed 28 February 2020.

Olufemi, Lola. (2020). *Feminism, Interrupted: Disrupting Power*. London: Pluto Press.

Palmer, Lisa Amanda. (2019). 'Diane Abbott, misogynoir and the politics of Black British feminism's anticolonial imperatives: "In Britain too, it's as if we don't exist".' *The Sociological Review*. https://doi.org/10.1177/0038026119892404.

Pegado, Briana. (2018). 'Briana Pegado: We are facing a cultural crisis if the creative industries do not become more diverse.' *Commonspace*. Last modified 10 August, https://www.commonspace.scot/articles/13133/briana-pegado-we-are-facing-cultural-crisis-if-creative-industries-do-not-become-more. Accessed 12 June 2019.

Rae, Mandla. (2020). 'Creative conversations: Black women artists making and doing—Institute for Black Atlantic Research, Preston.' *Corridor8*. Last modified 29 February. https://corridor8.co.uk/article/black-women-artists-making-and-doing. Accessed 29 February 2020.

Roberts, Carys & Emden, Joshua. (2019). 'Editorial.' *IPPR Progressive Review* 26(2): 120–124. https://doi.org/10.1111/newe.12161.

Roberts, Sarah. T. (2019). *Behind the Screen: Content Moderation in the Shadows of Social Media*. New Haven and London: Yale University Press.

Saha, Anamik. (2018). *Race and the Cultural Industries*. Cambridge: Polity Press.

Salty. (2019). 'Exclusive: An investigation into algorithmic bias in content policing on Instagram (PDF download).' *Salty*, https://saltyworld.net/algorithmicbiasreport-2. Accessed 19 December 2019.

Sobande, Francesca. (2017). 'Watching me watching you: Black women in Britain on YouTube.' *European Journal of Cultural Studies* 20(6): 655–671. https://doi.org/10.1177/1367549417733001.

Sobande, Francesca. (2019a). 'Memes, digital remix culture and (re)mediating British politics and public life.' *IPPR Progressive Review* 26(2): 151–160. https://doi.org/10.1111/newe.12155.

Sobande, Francesca. (2019b). 'Woke-washing: "Intersectional' femvertising and branding 'woke' bravery.' *European Journal of Marketing*, Vol. ahead-of-print No. ahead-of-print. https://doi.org/10.1108/EJM-02-2019-0134.

Sobande, Francesca, Fearfull, Anne & Brownlie, Douglas. (2019). 'Resisting media marginalisation: Black women's digital content and collectivity.' *Consumption Markets & Culture*. https://doi.org/10.1080/10253866.2019.1571491.

Sobande, Francesca & Krys, Osei. (2020). '*An African City*: Black women's creativity, pleasure, diasporic (dis)connections and resistance through aesthetic and media practices and scholarship.' *Communication, Culture & Critique*, tcz024. https://doi.org/10.1093/ccc/tcaa016.

Sobande, Francesca. (2020a). 'Between digital labour, leisure and liberation.' *Journalism, Media and Culture: The Official JOMEC School Blog—Commentary, Debate and Opinion*. Last modified 13 February, https://www.jomec.co.uk/blog/between-digital-labour-leisure-and-liberation. Accessed 13 February 2020.

Sobande, Francesca. (2020b). 'Creative work, community and support in a time of crisis.' *Creative Cardiff*. Last modified 20 March, https://www.creativecardiff.org.uk/news/creative-work-community-and-support-time-crisis. Accessed 20 March 2020.

Spare Rib Collective. (1988). 'Black women artists.' *Spare Rib* 1988(188): 8–12.

Spelic, Sherri. (2019). *Care at the Core: Conversational Essays on Identity, Education and Power*. Hamburg, Germany: Monica C. LoCascio of Make Books Happen & Sebastian Kaltenbrunner.

Steele, Catherine Knight. (2016a). 'The digital barbershop: Blogs and online oral culture within the African American community.' *Social Media + Society* 2(4): 1–10. https://doi.org/10.1177/2056305116683205.

Steele, Catherine Knight. (2016b). 'Signifyin', bitching, and blogging: Black women and resistance discourse online.' In *The Intersectional Internet: Race, Sex, Class, and Culture Online*, edited by Safiya Umoja Noble & Brendesha M. Tynes, pp. 73–93. New York: Peter Lang.

Steele, Catherine Knight. (2017). 'Black bloggers and their varied publics: The everyday politics of black discourse online.' *Television & New Media* 19(2): 112–127. https://doi.org/10.1177/1527476417709535.

Sulter, Maud. (1985). *As a Blackwoman*. London: Akira.

Sulter, Maud & Pollard, Ingrid. (eds.) (1990). *Passion: Discourses on Blackwomen's Creativity*. London: Urban Fox Press.

Tajudeen, Bolanle & Silveira, Cynthia. (2018). 'Black Blossoms: The black female artists you should be following.' *Virgin*. Last modified 17 August, https://www.virgin.com/entrepreneur/black-blossoms-black-female-artists-you-should-be-following. Accessed 7 January 2020.

Tate, Shirley Anne. (2009). *Black Beauty: Aesthetics, Stylization, Politics.* Farnham: Ashgate Publishing.

Tate, Shirley Anne. (2017a). *The Governmentality of Black Beauty Shame: Discourse, Iconicity and Resistance.* Basingstoke: Palgrave Macmillan.

Tate, Shirley Anne. (2017b). 'Skin: Post-feminist bleaching culture and the political vulnerability of blackness.' In *Aesthetic Labour: Rethinking Beauty Politics in Neoliberalism*, edited by Ana Sofia Elias, Rosalind Gill & Christina Scharff, pp. 199–213. Basingstoke: Palgrave Macmillan.

Thompson, Selina. (2017). 'Excerpts from the diary of a Black Woman at the Edinburgh Fringe.' *Exeunt Magazine.* Last modified 21 August, http://exeuntmagazine.com/features/excerpts-diary-black-woman-edinburgh-fringe. Accessed 18 August 2018.

Tilly, Lisa & Shilliam, Robbie. (2018). 'Raced markets: An introduction.' *New Political Economy* 23(5): 534–543. https://doi.org/10.1080/13563467.2017.1417366.

Uzor, Tia-Monique. (2019). 'Coming to movement: African diasporic women in British dance.' In *To Exist is to Resist: Black Feminism in Europe*, edited by Akwugo Emejulu & Francesca Sobande, pp. 259–272. London: Pluto Press.

Williams, Keisha. (2018). 'Occupying unapologetically: *Friday Late: gal-dem*— Radical trust and co-production at the Victoria and Albert Museum, London.' In *Accessibility, Inclusion, and Diversity in Critical Event Studies*, edited by Rebecca Finkel, Briony Sharp & Majella Sweeney, pp. 93–106. New York: Routledge.

CHAPTER 4

Black Women's Digital Diaspora, Collectivity, and Resistance

Abstract This chapter highlights issues to do with Black digital diasporic content and communication. It discusses how Black women's digital activity can enable them to deal with experiences of oppression that are specific to their lives and in communal ways. This chapter explores resistant credentials of some of the digital experiences of Black women in Britain, while reckoning with potentially conflicting aspects of countercultural practices which exist in the context of digital consumerism. This discussion features analysis of how Black American popular and digital culture contributes to some of the digital encounters and lives of Black women in Britain in impactful ways. Overall, this chapter focuses on Black women's experiences of knowledge-sharing online, including via natural hair video blogs (vlogs) on YouTube.

Keywords Black women · Digital diaspora · Resistance · Social media · Vlog · YouTube

The twenty-first century is marked by the impact of globalisation and technology's significant role in cross-cultural communication which involves digital dialogue between individuals in different parts of the world—including Black people who connect with one another online. Streams of content and detailed discourse accompanying popular hashtags

© The Author(s) 2020
F. Sobande, *The Digital Lives of Black Women in Britain*,
Palgrave Studies in (Re)Presenting Gender,
https://doi.org/10.1007/978-3-030-46679-4_4

such as #NaijaTwitter and #GrowingUpBlack exemplify how Black people across the globe communicate and create online in ways inextricably connected to cues, references, and in-jokes that relate to the intricacies of their racial, ethnic, and cultural identities. However, arguably, hashtags themselves do not simply catalyse a sense of sociality, collectivity, or community. Rather, hashtags are used as part of the expression of relational Black diasporic dynamics which are not dependent on Twitter but can be enabled by it.

Prior research and writing demonstrates the societally impactful nature of the digital work, creativity, commentaries, practices, and encounters of Black people (Brock et al. 2010; Chatman 2017; Florini 2019; Gabriel 2016; Gray 2015; Hobson 2008; Johnson 2018; Jones 2019; McMillan Cottom 2017; Mohammed 2019; Noble and Tynes 2016; Nyabola 2018; Phelps-Ward and Laura 2016; Sharma 2013; Victoria 2020; Wheeler 2019). Major research on Black digital experiences includes the race, gender, media, and communication scholarship of Catherine Knight Steele (2016a, b, 2017) which highlights how digital spaces can become sites of oral communication that aid Black people's formation of alternate publics, used to 'critique the dominant culture, foster resistance' (Steele 2016a, p. 1) and develop counter-hegemonic discourse.

The extensive work of I'Nasah K. Crockett (2014)—writer, artist, and indie public scholar of Black performance, culture, politics, and history—highlights the prevalence of anti-Blackness and misogynoir on social media (Bailey 2010, Bailey and Trudy 2018), while connecting this to the history of Black women's oppression. Furthermore, the paramount research of film and media studies scholar Anna Everett (2009), sociologist and African American studies scholar Ruha Benjamin (2019), communication studies scholars Meredith D. Clark (2014), Sarah J. Jackson (2016), Safiya Umoja Noble (2018), Jessica H. Lu and Catherine Knight Steele (2019), Black digital studies scholar André Brock (2020), and race, media, and politics scholar Charlton D. McIlwain (2020)—among others—elucidates much about digital technology, online culture, and the lives of Black people.

Drawing on such work, particularly Everett's (2009) germinal book *Digital Diaspora: A Race for Cyberspace*, as well as the research of women's, gender, and sexuality studies scholar Janell Hobson (2008) which explores 'gendered and racial constructions of digital technology' (p. 112), this chapter focuses on the diasporic, collective, and, sometimes, resistant dimensions of the digital experiences of Black women in Britain.

Extant research examines 'the production of the self in the digital age through its troubled and unsettling relationship with the mirror and the screen as artefacts of self-production' (Ibrahim 2018, p. 1). Associated issues are considered in this chapter as part of discussion of how digital experiences can contribute to Black women's formation and affirmation of their identities, including, in some cases, when 'tuning into the video blogs (vlogs) of Black women in the US, to learn more about [Black Lives Matter] BLM, Black-owned businesses, and to gain consumer tips that are specific to them' (Sobande et al. 2019, p. 8).

The politics and lives of Black women are 'too often erased from or misrecognised in the European imagination' (Emejulu and Sobande 2019, p. 3). Hence, sections of this chapter consider how both the specific socio-political context of Britain and the influence of US popular culture—that is, African-American popular culture—shapes the digital experiences and lives of Black women in Britain. In addition, there is reflection on how such women's digital encounters can involve connecting with Black diasporic lives elsewhere, while navigating associated experiences of relationality and a politics of difference.

DIGITAL BLACKNESS, BORDERS, AND A POLITICS OF DIFFERENCE

Borders—barriers between one place and another, (de)constructed differences between people and cultures, containers, confinement, separations and edges, to be near or adjacent to, limits placed upon the contents of something, somewhere, or someone. Borders—invisible and tangible, felt and (re)imagined, enforced and challenged, reproduced and recreated, online and offline. Conceptualising the borders of experiences of Black identity and digital space has led to me questioning what constitutes a border and how borders, and perceptions of them, impact issues to do with Black lives in cyberspace and their surrounding political landscapes.

The creation and maintenance of literal and imagined borders between an 'us' and 'them' forms a key part of politics—globally, nationally, and locally. International relations are often rooted in decision-making concerning borders—whether it be the development of 'new' ones, the maintenance of existing borders, or the perceived dismantling of them. While it is far from being uncontained and borderless, media can be a means for messages and people to appear to or feel as though they transcend borders—even if ephemerally—by communicating with others in different geo-cultural locations and time zones. Still, the digital experiences of Black people are far from being borderless. They are shaped by physical and virtual geographies and many layers of power and politics.

Black people's digital experiences are affected by issues regarding language, interpretation and translation, censorship and control, access to the internet and digital technology, as well as the continued globally dominant position of much North American, European, and Anglocentric discourse in relation to ideas about Black identity and Black diaspora (Sobande and Osei 2020). Contrary to essentialist ideas about Black people which deny the existence of stark differences between their identities, cultures, perspectives, and lives, Black digital diasporic dialogue is contoured by Black people's disconnections and differences, as well as connections and commonalities. Often, discussions to do with Black diaspora and borders focus on issues to do with geography, culture, ethnicity, and constructions of the nation-state. What I comment on in my book concerns these matters but is also intended to contribute to conversations about the borders of social media and digital spaces—from the hypervisibility of discussions on Twitter, to the ways that content created there moves into and across other online and offline environments.

In other words, how do the digital experiences of Black women in Britain involve navigating the borders of Black identity, geographies, and digital contexts which are constructed, contained, and constrained in ways that may contemporaneously enable and hamper meaningful articulations and expressions of Black life? How are Black diasporic experiences—including who has the 'right' to 'claim' them—expressed and contested as part of the digital encounters of Black women in Britain? How can acknowledging differences and disagreements within Black diasporic discussions—including digital ones—aid understandings of contemporary Black lives?

(How) are the digital experiences of Black people bordered, and with what effects? What is a 'global' Black digital 'voice', and does, could, or should one even exist? To what extent might forms of digital Blackness involve online experiences that overcome borders, and politics which is 'inclusive' of all Black lives? What does 'inclusive' mean in this case and is it a useful concept? I do not claim to have answers to all of these questions, nor do I suggest that such questions can be neatly answered at all, but throughout the course of the following sections is a discussion of how the digital experiences of Black women in Britain can involve both pushing against and reinforcing various borders—in ways that are symptomatic of global hierarchies, Anglocentrism, and the hegemony of the US and Britain. Considering these issues pertaining to power and global relations is imperative as part of this work, including because 'diaspora, as a social formation, is simultaneously framed by relationships of domination and is itself a structured hierarchy' (Makalani 2009, p. 1).

BLACK DIGITAL DIALOGUE BETWEEN BRITAIN AND THE US

When interviewing Black women in Britain about their digital habits and encounters, Facebook, YouTube, Twitter and Instagram were all mentioned as providing an opportunity to learn about each other's lives while also discussing their experiences online with Black people in the US. Related digital dialogue spurred on by a Black diasporic politics of difference includes conversations regarding how politics in the US and Britain compares. The politics of difference that plays out and is played with as part of Black women's digital activities also includes conversations concerning similarities and differences between understandings and experiences of Black identity and anti-Blackness in Britain and the US.

Nobody I interviewed disputed the notion that white supremacy and anti-Black racism is global, yet, can manifest in different ways across geographies. Instead, when interviewing Black women in Britain there was discussion of how through participating in Black diasporic conversations on social media they had learnt more about different, but, related histories, forms of white supremacy, and contemporary experiences of Black life—particularly in the US and Britain. In the words of one woman who I spoke to, who is in her thirties, moved to Britain from the US years ago, and chose the comical pseudonym Dr Diddly Doo:

> I will say that before I came here, I was curious to know what was the Black woman's experience in the UK and what will I find? I knew there were Black women there but are there generations and generations of Black people to the point that they're like 'I'm Black and British', or their parents migrated from other parts of the world so they're like 'I'm Black Jamaican British'? What you see on TV is not the Black British experience...I think that the only person I could name who people would be like 'oh yeah!' is Idris Elba. A lot of people don't have a concept [of Blackness] beyond the American borders.

Such comments were made as part of a wider conversation about how Dr Diddly Doo uses social media to connect and communicate with Black women in Britain and the US. That discussion included her reflecting on how due to the patriarchal and heteronormative nature of society, most teaching in school and public discourse concerning Black history in both places focuses on the words and work of cisgender heterosexual Black men. Turning to social media and digital spaces can be a prime way for Black women in Britain to learn about and share knowledge regarding Black herstories there (Akpan 2018; Folorunso 2018a, b; Sobande 2017) and around the world—including the relationship between Black women's experiences in Britain and the US (Sobande et al. 2019).

When discussing the intricacies of geographical boundaries that are internal to Britain, Dr Diddly Doo said:

> I mean…Britain is an island. It's a little small island [laughs], know what I mean?… and people need to be able to access other people, so there's an opportunity for that [online], especially for British Black women to be able to expand beyond the borders of Britain, especially in places like Scotland and Northern Ireland where you are quite isolated from the rest of what is happening.

The words of Dr Diddly Doo indicate 'the situatedness of the disembodied cyberself' (Kolko et al. 2000, p. 6)—which is always tethered to, and, by, different geographies and their borders and boundaries. Dr Diddly Doo's words also signal that although social media presents an opportunity for Black people in one continent to communicate with those in another, it can also support connections, conversations, and, potentially, the formation or strengthening of community between Black people in different parts of the one country. Black life, online and offline, can be influenced by internal national and regional power relations, as well as global hierarchical ones. Thus, efforts to conceptualise forms of digital Blackness beyond borders necessitate a concern with local, as well as national and global issues—all of which connect to the (in)visibility and hyper-visibility of different Black people, their experiences, and the politics of representation.

As the only Black woman in Britain I interviewed who is American, Dr Diddly Doo shared many examples of how she uses social media to communicate with Black women in the US and to keep abreast of news and politics there, while also attempting to minimise the potentially traumatic impact of her efforts to stay informed:

> It's very easy to filter people out on social media for me...especially with 'mute'...right now the US 2020 elections are happening and there's people putting stuff up and I'll mute them...and I've had arguments with people on social media before and it's never been satisfying, so I'm like 'nah, nah', I don't engage with that space...what I'll do with Facebook, in particular, is follow businesses and organisations that I want to hear from...filter out negative news...police brutality...focusing on things that I want to see.

Despite transnational qualities of Black people's digital experiences (Everett 2009; Sobande et al. 2019; Sobande and Osei 2020), there are also distinctly national, regional, and local elements which reflect how Black identities—even when re-embodied online—are linked to specific geo-cultural contexts and languages. For example, all of the Black digital diasporic experiences of the women who I interviewed involved them primarily, if not, solely, communicating in English; ultimately limiting the extent to which such experiences can be regarded as global or transnational, as opposed to Anglocentric and predominantly 'Western'.

Borders, or, perhaps, boundaries, that exist between understandings and experiences of Blackness as embodied and expressed by individuals in Britain and the US were a source of lots of discussion among the women who I interviewed. One specific example of this was the different parameters within which Black identity is defined. The 'one drop' rule that has moulded notions of race and Black identity in the US (Dagbovie-Mullins 2013) was a point of contention for 7 of the Black women in Britain who I interviewed, and illustrates the need to explore 'differences between America and England...in how race figures in the two societies' (Hall cited in hooks and Hall 2018, p. 31).

Conversations that unfolded during my interviews with Black women in Britain included critiques of the potential for 'mixed-race' identities to be 'reductively' equated with Blackness—in both the US and Britain—in ways that fail to account for colourism and how the Blackness of light-skinned and 'mixed-race' individuals is often societally favoured, so their treatment sharply contrasts with the systemic oppression of dark-skinned Black people. Associated online discussions and disagreements reflect issues that are explored in-depth as part of communication, American ethnic studies, gender, women, and sexuality studies scholar Ralina

L. Joseph's (2012) central work on 'transcending Blackness', which sheds light on how ideas concerning Black identity and post-racial politics are projected onto 'multiracial' individuals.

Some of the women who I spoke to highlighted how Black diasporic conversations on social media have provided them with the chance to learn about and discuss different geo-culturally specific histories and understandings of Black identity, including perceived (dis)connections between 'mixed-race' and Black identities in different parts of the world (Sims and Njaka 2019). Therefore, although digital spaces can be sites where Black people appear to overcome geographical borders and connect with each other across continents, such experiences may involve commentaries that uphold or contest other types of conceptual borders, or, boundaries—such as the perceived ones of Black identity, as constructed, deconstructed, and reconstructed by and through different people, politics, and places.

The critical race, communication, technology, and cyberspace work of Kolko et al. (2000) establishes that 'race matters in cyberspace precisely because all of us who spend time online are already shaped by the ways in which race matters offline, and we can't help but bring our own knowledge, experiences, and values with us when we log on' (pp. 4-5). The digital experiences of Black women who I interviewed occur within a landscape linked to the racial and racist politics of both Britain and the US, which is punctuated by the longstanding public condoning of white supremacist ideologies and the normalisation of discourses of so-called 'racial purity'. As such, those who I interviewed spoke about some of the ways that the perceived 'authenticity' of a person's Black identity may be questioned and critiqued as part of their digital experiences (Maragh 2017), in ways that reflect context-dependent ideas about Black identity, 'racial purity' and how the boundaries of Blackness are (re)presented and (re)constructed online. What does the notion of being 'authentically' Black mean, how does the concept of authenticity function in this context, and in what ways is this notion of being 'authentically' Black operationalised in digital spaces? Questions such as these linger.

Many of the experiences of those who I spoke to were indicative of how some 'Black women in Britain relationally engage with the digital content and commentaries of Black people in the US, including in ways that can foster their identification with the global Black Lives Matter (BLM) social justice movement, as well as their adoption of phrases associated with African American Vernacular English (AAVE)' (Sobande et al. 2019, pp. 6–7). Due to the distinctly scarce media coverage of BLM in mass-media in Britain, for many who I spoke to, social media had become the means through which they learnt about the movement, its development, and Black liberationist struggles in other countries. More precisely, 'the multi-level community and network building process commonly referred to as "Black Twitter"' (Clark 2014, p. x) was a strong source of their digital dialogue with Black people in the US.

Temi, who is in her twenties and is a researcher based in Scotland, referenced the significance of Black Twitter in her life and how she learns about Black lives and struggles in the US, when she said:

> In America, to do with Black Lives Matter…now it's coming back into the news over here [UK] but when it first happened, with like Trayvon Martin and Sandra Bland, it really wasn't over in the UK news that much. It wasn't featured at all. It's only now that it's really been featured.

The experiences of Temi and most of the women who I interviewed were reflective of how 'some Black women in Britain feel more connected to digital discussions led by Black online users in the US, than ideas and identities documented in British mass-media' (Sobande et al. 2019, p. 8). Another Black woman who I interviewed, named Annie, who is in her late teens and is an undergraduate student in England, spoke about her use of Lipstick Alley—a website which on Google Play is marketed as being about 'News, Sports, Celebrity Gossip from an African American perspective'. When speaking about Lipstick Alley, Annie said:

> It's a Black forum for African American women…I mean, it's not as good as it used to be back in the day, 'cause they used to have quite a few trolls…I guess because I found it at aged probably 14 or 15, and they just have every forum. The forum has like every alley you could think about, from politics to Black Lives Matter, to beauty, to celebrity gossip, to this, to that, to everything, and then they used to have a lot of 'tea spillers' as they'd say…so people who'd work in the industries, who would drop some gossip and they'd say either 'you can sip it' or 'you can spit it out'…but some of the things that they said did come true and you had a lot of insightful things on there. Through that, I became quite aware of you know, groups like…you know, where to buy Black-owned makeup and jewellery and you know, some of these TV shows. They would tell you about it. Like, 'this one is coming out, look out for it' and 'this one's quite good and look out for this'…so it means that you really get an in-depth

idea of what's going on around you and where to pick and choose…people giving their own experiences and different things, so that's quite helpful as well.

From discussing their participation in conversations on Lipstick Alley, to their thoughts on shows on Black & Sexy TV, and a myriad of Black-led podcasts (Barner and Sacrée 2020; Florini 2019), those who I interviewed shared many examples of how Black women in Britain are making use of digital spaces and social media to access and contribute to content and conversations that stem from the work and words of Black people in the US—especially, Black women. Still, there was also recognition of debates and disagreements that can occur between Black people online, as part of what five of the women who I spoke to affectionately, but, pointedly, referred to as being 'diaspora wars'.

In the words of Transatlantic Ghanaian fashion culture scholar Krys Osei (2019), to be a Black woman can be to experience 'indescribable joy, indescribable pain' (p. 742)—with such pain fuelled by the effects of co-dependent sexism, misogyny, and anti-Blackness. The insightful work of Jessica H. Lu and Catherine Knight Steele (2019) illustrates how social media is used by Black individuals in ways that involve 'asserting Black people's full humanity and range of emotion' (p. 831). In agreement with this position, and when reflecting on the experiences of those who I interviewed, it is clear that social media is used by Black women in Britain in ways that involve them expressing and learning about a range of experiences of Black identity and life, but which remain linked to the traits of different geo-cultural contexts.

Black Women's Natural Hair Vlogs and Knowledge-Sharing

One of the many online content-sharing sites where Black women in Britain seek out and source content created by, and depicting Black women, is YouTube—where 'various forms of cultural, social, and economic values are collectively produced by users *en masse*, via their consumption, evaluation, and entrepreneurial activities' (Burgess and Green 2009, p. 5). The YouTube experiences of Black women may reveal much about the 'subtleties and nuances of black women's lives' (Bobo 1995, p. 2) which are often dismissed and denied as part of derogatory media and public discourse about them.

Interviewing Black women in Britain about YouTube quickly gravitated to stories about their hair, including the Black beauty and hair vloggers they engage with. Natural hair journeys proved to be a nexus to issues concerning identity, authenticity, community and a sense of belonging. Contemporary shifts in the landscape of media platforms, especially, those enmeshed in digital culture, have altered power relations involved in producing and accessing on-screen images of Black people.

Frustrated with the lack of hairdressers in Scotland who cater to Black women, Temi took matters into her own hands and searched for natural haircare tips. She started sourcing YouTube content in 2010. Temi said:

> I wanted to understand how to look after my hair. That's what kicked it off. Now I follow so many people [on YouTube] and I literally take time out during the week. Like, I save videos and then just watch them...like whenever I've got a chance. It's something that I actively do.

Natural hair vlogs serve as a practical tool that enables Temi's self-education in terms of caring for natural African-Caribbean hair. On a more emotional level, they provide self-affirming experiences of feeling represented on-screen (Bobo 1995; Warner 2015). For Temi, television only offers restrictive images of Black women wearing 'wigs and weaves, Peruvian and Brazilian, and it doesn't seem like it is how Black women actually are'. Temi consistently made statements such as 'I want to see somebody who looks like me'. For this reason, she favours YouTube over television. Such engagement with the vlogs of Black women has been so influential that Temi has considered becoming a vlogger and was involved in establishing a natural hair collective. Temi indicates how engagement with the vlogs of Black women may include self-educational elements related to the diasporic identities of Black women in Britain.

Another woman who I interviewed, named Annie, spoke about her disinterest in YouTube when explaining why she still uses it to watch makeup tutorials. Annie said, 'with makeup, I can't watch one with white or...when I say Black women, it has to be dark-skinned Black women', who are infrequently depicted in mainstream makeup campaigns. Others who were interviewed made comparable comments:

> I think about what I need at the time, so my YouTube channels kind of guide me...I'll be like 'do I need to feel better about myself sometimes, emotionally, physically'...Trying to find makeup as a Black woman...it's

such an endeavor…sometimes you're like, 'I just want to find a good foundation!'…then you go on YouTube and someone goes 'oh, here you go' and that's that exchange that you're having with these people.

The remarks of some who I spoke to indicate that they sought out Black women's vlogs to gain more inclusive forms of advice which are glaringly absent in mainstream media and markets—especially at the point that I interviewed Temi and Annie, which was long before the launch of beauty brands such as Fenty by Rhianna. Their comments illustrate how highly practical needs and daily frustrations (tips and advice are abundantly available for light-skinned women) may segue into the ideological and political. YouTube is available to Black women in Britain as a socio-cultural source of knowledge shared among Black women. This is emphasised by the words of Okra, who is in her thirties and lives in Scotland:

> Try a mud or a clay wash…you'll be shocked at what your hair looks like afterwards. You understand why the ancestors used to do that…so much has been lost in transmission…I'm grateful that we are actively trying to remember how to do this, so that our children…the babies…are ok…don't have to go through this part anyway. It's a small thing but it's a big thing.

Throughout history, knowledge-networks have been 'passed down over generations of people' (Harrison III et al. 2015, p. 306), and which have 'come to represent the meaning of racial, ethnic, and cultural or national identities' (ibid.). Various ways that culturally specific information about Black women's haircare is transmitted have changed with the rise of online content-sharing platforms (Johnson 2013). To merely interpret the YouTube activity analysed as being an exchange of practical questions and advice would be to omit complex issues which link the practical and everyday care of the self to the ideological work involved in identity construction and community.

Turning to natural hair vlogs involves a process of supporting the endeavours of other Black women, as well as, I argue, potentially 'making connections, promoting human connectedness and community building' (van Dijck 2013, p. 201), within a Black digital diaspora (Everett 2009). The comments of Nymeria, who is an artist in her twenties in Scotland, affirm this:

Like many other Black women, I didn't really know what the hell to do with my hair, so it was amazing to find a community of natural hair gurus on YouTube. There are literally thousands and thousands of Black women in all these different parts of the world, doing this. We consider them beauty bloggers but I feel as if they live within their own little niche, which is particular to Black womanhood...some, they're just really small channels...and sometimes I just like to give a girl a chance, you know? ...it's kind of soothing to me at this point, because I've been doing it so long and I feel like it's such an amazing thing that we created that for ourselves.

Even passive participation in the comments section of Black women's vlogs can provide young Black women in Britain with a sense of belonging which may otherwise be hard to access when situated in predominantly white contexts. Rachel, who is in her twenties and is a recent graduate based in England remarked, 'you'll see stuff in the comment section and be like, "oh yeah! That's me too. That happens to me too." You can really relate'. Rachel's words illustrate how it is not simply the content of Black women's vlogs that yields relational experiences—it is also the commentary and sense of community they stimulate.

The comments of Dr Diddly Doo are a reminder of different types of collectivity that may be available to Black women online, and that the different beliefs and perspectives of Black women mean that not every space by Black women, and for them, will appeal or be open to all other Black women:

I remember...about a year ago...I got on some Facebook groups of different Black women and what I realised is that not all Black women are the same [laughs] and we don't all have the same opinions about things...really conservative Christian protestant people talking about...'you should be like this'...having altercations with people, including other Black women...so I started looking for other groups and had to learn how to expand that vocabulary of keywords for different people, so I've joined new groups and taken myself out of other ones.

Dr Diddly Doo also reflected on challenges involved in online dating as a Black woman (Adewunmi 2010). She said:

I will say one of the ways that I have made connections with people here has been digital media...talking to people and getting to know different people on dating sites. It was weird...I mean honestly [laughs]...I think there are always people who exoticise Black women...if you're anybody who is not white they're probably exoticising you some how...I find the internet to be a place where a lot of people will quite proudly wave their freak flags in a way that they probably wouldn't do in real life.

As Dr Diddly Doo emphasised, as she was one of relatively few Black women in the part of Scotland she was based in at that time, the hyper-visibility of being a Black woman in a predominantly white society mapped onto her digital experience of dating. Dr Diddly Doo laughed when speaking about how her and her friends who are Black women would share their experiences of online dating and would share tips on how to navigate the exoticisation that they encountered, and who to avoid on dating apps.

While praising how digital spaces can contribute to Black women's knowledge-production and knowledge-sharing, Dr Diddly Doo also spoke of what she feels are limitations of the construction of community and solidarity online.

> I think it can be overwhelming if you don't find a particular space that you do belong...but there are opportunities...if you're curious about technology and you're a Black woman you can go to an Afrotech women's group. Not just a space to talk and commiserate but to share opportunities. Having created spaces of solidarity, particularly for Black women before, I've noticed that sitting around a table and being able to talk to each other face to face is really critical and I just find...social media...that's not really how conversations work...that being said, I do think that what there is....is that people are finding their spaces.

Some of the sentiments captured by Dr Diddly Doo's comments connect to the potential to find and forge a sense of collectivity and communal space online, as identified and discussed by blogger, documentary producer, author, and scholar Renina Jarmon (2013) in *Black Girls Are From the Future: Essays On: Race, Digital Creativity and Pop Culture.*

Returning to a focus on YouTube, when speaking about her use of it, Temi detailed how vlogs provide the opportunity to learn from other Black women and Black people:

> I would even go as far as to say, on my YouTube subscription list there are very few white YouTubers I actually follow. I don't think that it is

anything to do with racism or being prejudiced in any way. I think it's just growing up I had never been taught by any Black teachers...all of my teachers at primary school up until high school. The very first time I was ever taught by an African or Black lecturer, it was one class. It was a lecturer at undergraduate and she was Black and it was like, wow! It was a massive deal. I just want to know more and learn more about what the history is and experiences are of people who look like me.

Miss Africa—who is in her twenties, involved in activist work and plans to train as a counsellor—had a slightly different story to offer that underlines both the practical and socio-political realms of such YouTube activity. Miss Africa lost her sight in recent months but spoke about how the importance of natural hair vlogs relates to much more than visual signification:

> My friends, when I was in hospital...used to play these videos for me because I like to listen to them, because even if you can't see them, you can hear what they use for their hair...which is quite nice because you need that.

Miss Africa's comments were some of many which involved implicit and sometimes explicit references to a sense of connection and solidarity. Miss Africa also spoke about her contrasting experience of listening to audio descriptions of televised media content in Scotland and expressed frustration at hearing Black women's hair described as 'bush' style. Her critique of such offensive audio descriptions of the appearance of Black women brings attention to the multifaceted ways that media constructions of Black women are impacted by entwined anti-Black racism and sexism—even audio descriptions intended to ensure the accessibility of content.

Unlike such media that she encounters on television in Scotland, natural hair vlogs which are created by Black women and which they narrate, provide Miss Africa with media experiences that not only include images of Black women, but which also foreground their perspectives as expressed in their own words. Like Temi, Nymeria and Miss Africa, Rachel alluded to this element of kinship when speaking of her love of natural hair vlogs:

> I just felt like...it's just nice to see...it sounds really bad but it's nice to see other people struggling like you, or going through the same stuff. Like,

growing up I'd say since secondary school...my secondary school was quite mixed in terms of race...but I could only think of one other Black girl that had natural hair, so I didn't have anyone to talk to about like...what it's like to care for natural hair. Like, saying 'oh yeah so I'm getting my hair done today' or 'what kind of grease do you use?' [laughs] random stuff like that.

It has been noted that 'black women's texts nourish and sustain their readers' (Bobo 1995, p. 6), and in the early twenty-first century, such texts include user-generated YouTube vlogs. Engaging with the vlogs of Black women has the capacity to become part of 'strategies of representation or empowerment' (Bhabha 1994, p. 2), such as by enabling self-affirming feelings and forms of collective self-education.

However, Black women's use of YouTube indicates how 'commodification is a process that is both enabling and constraining' (Saha 2012, p. 740). Plantain Baby, for example, who is in her twenties, is an artist, and is based in England, said, 'there's still a bit of an issue because Black people can produce any kind of content that they want [on YouTube] but the people that are behind YouTube and the film industry, it's still white dominated'. In addition, Dr Diddly Doo commented on the educational potential of YouTube as well as how it can result in the creation of content that ultimately feeds into mainstream media organisations which are predominantly led by white people:

> I know that some people say I went to the university of YouTube...I do think that traditional education can be quite dangerous for Black women sometimes. YouTube, I like to think I use it to find information and then I fall down the rabbit hole...open tabs...I think I've seen Black people depicted interestingly on YouTube as a way to get exposure, so Issa Rae and her Misadventures of Awkward Black Girl...that was one of the first of those things that I watched...what's it called?...webseries!..do people do these anymore?...oh yeah, they do but they charge for it now. I remember learning about crowdsourcing from it...I loved it and then I started getting into some other stuff...I don't know if it was I Am Other...I was able to watch everyday people put up funny stuff before they became big stars that had to fit into the media machine.

At the same time, for many of the women who I interviewed a key draw of the vlogs of Black women is the opportunity to see Black women in control of their depiction. Ola is in her late teens and based in Scotland,

and when speaking about Black women vloggers, she said: 'it's just great to see Black women being successful in the media I guess, yeah. They just have such great personalities as well and they offer so much advice online to other women'.

For Ola, the symbolic value of Black women's vlogs includes inspiration yielded by their success, regardless that the vlogs may also net the vloggers income (and thus suggest commercial or even mercenary interests). Relatedly, Nymeria said 'there's this amazing YouTuber I watch and who makes a lot of this stuff herself...she's not even asking for any money'. When explaining processes of communication, Hall (1993, p. 510) outlines that 'the degrees of "understanding" and "misunderstanding" in the communicative exchange—depend on the degrees of symmetry/asymmetry (relations of equivalence) established between the positions of the "personifications", encoder-producer and decoder-receiver'. Black women who are vloggers may be both the producer and subject of their vlogs. Regarding the experiences of the Black women who I interviewed, the visible agency and self-possession of Black women as content producers is a big part of the appeal of these vlogs.

(Medi)activist Sentiments

The online experiences of those who I interviewed may be viewed as an example of how Black women in Britain engage with 'alternative' media (Couldry and Curran 2003), rather than what is offered in mainstream mass-media in Britain. However, while talk of alternative images involves reflecting on media that 'provide divergent points of view and cultural choices' (Lievrouw 2011, p. 1) to those available in mainstream markets, such discussion is often associated more with news and current affairs than entertainment and lifestyle-based media. Moreover, the word 'alternative' does not fully capture the proactive, resistant, and political sentiments involved in the digital activities of some of the women who I interviewed. This includes how Okra spoke of turning to the online content of Black people, as part of efforts to 'decolonise my mind'. These ideological underpinnings of the digital activity of some Black women in Britain signal varying degrees of (medi)activism,[1] or, at the least, resistance.

Influenced by Dhaenens' (2012, p. 446) exploration of 'the resistant potentiality of texts' on YouTube, and in line with how vlogs can speak to Black women's sense of identity and self-esteem, '(medi)activist sentiments' as a concept can be used to grasp how the women who

I interviewed voiced their often implicit, yet ostensibly resistant media experiences. Comments made by Temi exemplify the active avoidance of mainstream mass-media in favour of YouTube:

> I don't necessarily watch TV anymore. Most of the TV that I watch is mainly YouTube channels. Essentially that's my new TV because it's content that I want to see, not content that is dictated by white, middle class and middle-aged men, who are trying to figure out what the majority would maybe like. Then, when you say that you're going with what the majority would maybe like, minorities are always left out.

Temi, as do the others, frames the importance of her use of YouTube by detailing some of the everyday and structural racism (Emejulu and Bassel 2015; Essed 1991) Black women in Britain commonly experience:

> In the 90s there weren't that many other Black people around you [in Scotland]…if you got on a bus, you were often the only Black person on a bus and people wouldn't necessarily want to sit next to you. That's what you feel. People would be standing and literally, it happened to me so many times. I'd be on the bus going to primary school and no one would want to sit next to me, even though the seat was there…it affected me, yes. Not having that access to other people who look like you…you crave it more, so you end up closer to the sort of Black or African side. The identity that you feel that you ascribe to…it becomes okay. This is the way that I see myself…that's exactly what happened with me. In high school we talked about the Jacobites, Mary Queen of Scots, yeah [laughs] and there was no Black history…I was fighting…resistance to not just be the status quo and let that be my identity, knowing that there was so much more to me…I went and found that for myself…actively seeking specific mediums that actually relate to who I am…because the depiction of Black people on TV in the UK is very few and far between.

Seeking out images of Black women on YouTube thus becomes about more than finding practical advice. It is part of a shift from implicit, underground unease to a more openly political stance. This may range from being critical of mainstream television to 'fighting' the absence of Black history, as Temi does by sourcing specific vlogs. Seeking out the vlogs of Black women can be stimulated by entertainment-based motivations, but can also be a very openly resistant online activity. This can involve the (medi)activist sentiment of trying to 'strengthen one's identity', as Temi puts it, while facing discrimination and having limited opportunities to learn from Black people first-hand.

Although the remarks of others who I interviewed are more general, similar patterns can be discerned. For instance, Jennifer, who is in her twenties and is a student in England, speaks about dismissing televised images because she feels they (mis)represent Black women: 'Actually I would say, instead of television, I tend to watch YouTube videos more. There's you know, with YouTube videos, you tend to get people more representative of yourself...cause it's just any person can go on there and make content that's more truthful'. When considering Jennifer's remarks, especially in the years since this interview, I find myself thinking about the duality of YouTube—it can be used by Black women in ways that enrich their lives, yet, it is also a video-sharing platform that is rife with far-right content and vlogs framed as being 'factual' and 'truthful' but which propagate falsities and hate speech.

As Black feminist, scholar, and activist hooks (1992, 1995, 2009, 2014) observes, Black people have in both the past and present challenged how we are presented in mass-media. Traditional examples of resistance include public protests, boycotts and 'turning off the television set' (hooks 1992, 1995). Rather than discount the resistant and oppositional intention (Bobo 1995; hooks 1992, 1995) of simple acts such as choosing not to watch television, I prefer to follow hooks' lead and include this form of everyday political protest. This preference is undergirded by the fact that in the interviews, Black women talked about the wide range of their YouTube use. They specifically included how they search for and view content by Black women activists, unearthing further ways that their YouTube use involves (medi)activist sentiments.

Plantain Baby also emphasised how mainstream mass-media primarily promote white and heteronormative identities (Bobo 1995; Dhaenens 2012; Hall 2003) that Black women may not relate to:

> There are loads of Black queer women here but there's not space for us [in mainstream media] which is maybe one of the reasons why you don't hear about us enough...because we're having to do things on our own.

Engagement with YouTube videos created by and featuring Black women can provide Black women viewers with a stronger sense of ownership over their media spectator experiences. Shelby, who is in her twenties and is based in England, summarised this when saying, 'I think it's about going out of my own way, looking for my own sort of media, looking for what I want to see, or like…looking for people that I can really relate to'. Additionally, Plantain Baby hinted at ideologically influenced reasons behind her dismissal of television:

> I haven't watched television properly in years. I mean, as a Black person, there's nothing really entertaining. There's nothing there that references anything to do with my Blackness. If anything, it's going to be on the news in some sort of negative way…I kind of don't pay attention to the media but I would say, do they even think Black British women even exist here? You know, is that even an identity to explore? I also feel like there is a constant negative stigma and stereotypes about Black women. There is a lot of misrepresentation. A lot of unreliable sources. The people who are recording these Black experiences are not Black! They're not Black women! You're not hearing from the horse's mouth.

Plantain Baby is involved in a creative collective that shares the narratives of Black women in Britain and, as part of that collective, has produced YouTube content. Still, YouTube does not exist outside of capitalism, white supremacy, or patriarchy, as Plantain Baby pointed out. To conceive of digital 'technology as innocent or neutral misunderstands the social relations of technology and its very real material consequences in our social world' (Emejulu and McGregor 2016, p. 1). In addition, taking a political stance and protesting against discrimination and exclusion can take a wide variety of forms. It would not do to overlook the range of ways that those who I interviewed are critical and seek alternatives to mainstream media, in order to construct their identities and build a sense of community. However, '[t]his is not to suggest that all Black women interpret media in the same and critical way' (Sobande et al. 2019, p. 11).

Racism 'scars symbol making and the cultural industries that disseminate information and entertainment to audiences' (Hesmondhalgh and Saha 2013, p. 179). Content generated by YouTube vloggers is typically 'situated at a crossroads between the popular and the margins' (Dhaenens 2012, p. 444) which those who I interviewed feel is fertile ground for the spectatorship of images of Black women, created for and by them. Some of the experiences that those who I interviewed discuss reveal watching YouTube to be an ideologically charged activity that relates directly to experiences of disconnection and exclusion, as well as, I argue, the opportunity to explore 'the possibility of engaging knowledge across different kinds of boundaries' (hooks cited in hooks and Hall 2018, p. 6)—online and offline. While living in Britain, Ola, who is in her late teens and based in Scotland sources images of Black women on YouTube, and connects this with the African diasporic element of her identity. When in Nigeria, Ola does not feel an impetus to actively seek out images of Black women on-screen:

> Well when I was younger...well, we were in Nigeria so there was lots of Black women on TV. Yeah, because of all the Nollywood films and shows and stuff like that, so yeah it was a normal thing I guess. It was when I came here [UK] that I realised that it wasn't so...like, not normal...but it wasn't often that you'd see a Black woman on TV when I came here.

Online platforms provide enabling forms of technology here. Film and media studies scholar Anna Everett (2009, p. 20) asserts that since 1995, there have been 'swelled ranks of black people throughout the African diaspora connecting to the Internet' and through it. Ola is eager to remain connected to a Black African experience, and keeping up with the vlogs of Black women is one way of doing so. Plantain Baby also emphasised how content-sharing platforms facilitate such a sense of connection: 'I feel like you are able to see and kind of understand narratives from different Black people all over the world. It is an outlet for Black people in the diaspora to talk about their experiences and share their narratives'. Overall, many of the interviews in this regard speak to the 'subversive capacity' of Black women as media spectators in the twenty-first century context of online YouTube habits, as Bobo (1995, p. 5) maintained earlier in relation to movies, novels, and other content carriers.

Concluding Thoughts

Commonalities across the interviews point to a pattern in how Black women make sense of their representation in mainstream media, versus certain videos of Black women vloggers. The difference lies between the exclusion and neglect yielded by mainstream media, and the opportunity to engage in resistant and self-empowering activity when building an identity influenced by the online voices of other Black women. Being a Black woman in predominantly white places will often involve dealing with everyday anti-Black racism and striving for a sense of belonging. This does not directly or immediately translate into a political stance. Digital habits can appear to be more coincidental than intentional, due to how YouTube recommends videos, and what happens to be on the social media profiles of friends. That said, the digital habits of many who I spoke to, including their engagement with images of Black women on YouTube, were often purposeful and encouraged by feelings of marginalisation, that participation in a Black digital diaspora (Everett 2009) was felt as remedying.

To return to the words of Rachel, 'I could only think of one other Black girl that had natural hair, so I didn't have anyone to talk to about like...what it's like to care for natural hair'. For Black women in Britain, YouTube allows the perusing and production of images of Black women as a means of self-actualisation, self-care and support. Evidently, the proliferation of content-sharing platforms will make how some diasporic people connect with each other increasingly digital in nature. As ever, more research 'that can illuminate and enrich our understanding of the social formation of black identity' (hooks 2014, p. 8), as well as 'the commodification of "blackness" is needed' (ibid.). During the early stages of my research I saw little evidence of this commodification in the natural hair vlogs discussed in the interviews, but such vlogs have increasingly become an interesting business proposition for product manufacturers and other businesses, particularly as 'the desire to market Black hair care products and services on these various venues, with such enormous access, is quite popular in the twenty-first century' (Johnson 2013, p. 79).

Further studies of how Black women's online activity influences mainstream media, last but not least, can play an important part in challenging the 'lack of attention to race and ethnicity in the booming research field of cultural production studies' (Hesmondhalgh and Saha 2013, p. 179) in Britain. Online platforms such as YouTube will feed mainstream television, yet restrictions apply there. As Dhaenens (2012) observes, 'where the margins allow more freedom, the popular is submitted to social and cultural conventions' (pp. 444–445).

Therefore, when Black women in Britain want to see images of Black women that are rarely represented, for the time being, their chances are much better when they turn to YouTube vlogs than when switching on the television. Such alternative images will be crafted and sought out by Black women in Britain in many ways, ranging from accidentally to actively and ambitiously. Regardless of this diversity of strategies and tactics, the vlogs of Black women have become connected with the identity formation and community building of Black women in Britain, some of whom are creating and carving out their own media experiences and, in turn, themselves.

NOTE

1. This chapter draws on material included in my article 'Watching me watching you: Black women in Britain on YouTube.' *European Journal of Cultural Studies* (2017) 20(6): 655–671. https://doi.org/10.1177/1367549417733001. In addition, it draws on material included in Sobande, Francesca, Fearfull, Anne & Brownlie, Douglas. (2019). 'Resisting media marginalisation: Black women's digital content and collectivity.' *Consumption Markets & Culture*. https://doi.org/10.1080/10253866.2019.1571491. In the months and years since these articles were published, I have become more skeptical concerning the radical and resistant potentials of much digital and media activity—particularly due to the steep and stifling constraints of capitalism. Therefore, although I include the terms '(medi)activism' and '(medi)activist sentiments' (Sobande 2017) in this chapter, I do so cautiously. Furthermore, I 'maintain the position that Black women's marketplace and media choices and production can be political, and, at times, involve struggling against their/our oppression' (Sobande and Osei 2020, p. 15) but I 'remain critical of claims that reductively equate Black women's liberation with their consumer culture activities' (ibid.). Thus, I continue to question the radical and resistant scope of actions and exchanges embedded within capitalist marketplace settings and infrastructures, while also being conscious of the many creative, collective, and digital ways that Black women are 're-imagining blackness and womanhood beyond technological exclusion and surveillance' (Hobson 2008, p. 111), and are pushing against and attempting to dismantle structural power relations that breed inequalities.

REFERENCES

Adewunmi, Bim. (2010). 'Racism and online dating: My experience.' *The Guardian*. Last modified 28 October, https://www.theguardian.com/lifeandstyle/2010/oct/28/racism-and-online-dating. Accessed 7 November 2019.

Akpan, Paula. (2018). 'Social media has taught me more about black British history than I ever learned in school—and that's a crying shame.' *The Independent*. Last modified 7 October, https://www.independent.co.uk/voices/black-history-month-social-media-nottingham-race-riots-reni-eddo-lodge-claudia-jones-martin-luther-a8572701.html. Accessed 15 June 2019.

Bailey, Moya. (2010). 'They aren't talking about me ...' *Crunk Feminist Collective*. Last modified 14 March, http://www.crunkfeministcollective.com/2010/03/14/they-arent-talking-about-me/. Accessed 28 March 2020.

Bailey, Moya & Trudy. (2018). 'On misogynoir: Citation, erasure, and plagiarism.' *Feminist Media Studies* 18(4): 762–768. https://doi.org/10.1080/14680777.2018.1447395.

Barner, Briana & Frangine, Sacrée. (2020). 'Safe and sound: How Podcasts became audio enclaves for Black women.' *Bitch Media*. Last modified 26 February, https://www.bitchmedia.org/article/podcasts-audio-enclaves-black-women. Accessed 26 February 2020.

Benjamin, Ruha. (2019). *Race After Technology: Abolitionist Tools for the New Jim Code*. Cambridge and Medford, MA: Polity Press.

Bhabha, Homi K. (1994). *The Location of Culture*. New York: Routledge.

Bobo, Jacqueline. (1995). *Black Women as Cultural Readers*. New York: Columbia University Press.

Brock, André. (2020). *Distributed Blackness: African American Cybercultures*. New York: New York University Press.

Brock, André, Kvasny, Lynette & Hayles, Kayla. (2010). 'Cultural appropriations of technical capital: Black women, weblogs, and the digital divide.' *Information, Communication & Society* 13(7): 1040–1059. https://doi.org/10.1080/1369118X.2010.498897.

Burgess, Jean & Green, Joshua. (2009). *YouTube: Online Video and Participatory Culture*. Cambridge and Malden, MA: Polity Press.

Chatman, Dayna. (2017). 'Black Twitter and the politics of viewing Scandal.' In *Fandom: Identities and Communities in a Mediated World* (2nd ed.), edited by Jonathan Gray, Cornel Sandvoss & C. Lee Harrington, pp. 299–314. New York: New York University.

Clark, Meredith D. (2014). 'To tweet our own cause: A mixed-methods study of the online phenomenon "Black Twitter".' Chapel Hill, NC: University of North Carolina at Chapel Hill Graduate School, 2014. https://doi.org/10.17615/7bfs-rp55.

Couldry, Nick & Curran, James. (eds.) (2003). *Contesting Media Power: Alternative Media in a Networked World*. Oxford: Rowman & Littlefield.

Crockett, I'Nasah. (2014). '"Raving Amazons": Antiblackness and misogynoir in social media.' *Model View Culture*. Last modified 30 June, https://modelviewculture.com/pieces/raving-amazons-antiblackness-and-misogynoir-in-social-media. Accessed 20 March 2020.

Dagbovie-Mullins, Sika A. (2013). *Crossing B(l)ack: Mixed-Race Identity in Modern American Fiction and Culture*. Knoxville: University of Tennessee Press.

Dhaenens, Frederik. (2012). 'Queer cuttings on YouTube: Re-editing soap operas as a form of fan-produced queer resistance.' *European Journal of*

Cultural Studies 15(4): 442–456. https://doi.org/10.1177/136754941244 2205.

Emejulu, Akwugo & Bassel, Leah. (2015). 'Minority women, austerity and activism.' *Race & Class* 57(2): 86–95. https://journals.sagepub.com/doi/ 10.1177/0306396815595913.

Emejulu, Akwugo & McGregor, Callum. (2016). 'Towards a radical digital citizenship in digital education.' *Critical Studies in Education* 60(1): 131–147. https://doi.org/10.1080/17508487.2016.1234494.

Emejulu, Akwugo & Sobande, Francesca. (eds.) (2019). *To Exist is to Resist: Black Feminism in Europe*. London: Pluto Press.

Essed, Philomena. (1991). *Understanding Everyday Racism: An Interdisciplinary Theory*. Newbury Park, CA: Sage.

Everett, Anna. (2009). *Digital Diaspora: A Race for Cyberspace*. Albany, NY: SUNY Press.

Florini, Sarah. (2019). *Beyond Hashtags: Racial Politics and Black Digital Networks*. New York: New York University Press.

Folorunso, Tomiwa. (2018a). 'Growing up Black in Scotland [video].' *BBC The Social*. Last modified 15 October, https://www.youtube.com/watch?reload= 9&v=WCzK2JkIodE. Accessed 9 June 2019.

Folorunso, Tomiwa. (2018b). 'Learning about Black Scottish history! [video].' *BBC The Social*. Last modified 23 October, https://www.bbc.co.uk/progra mmes/p06pnf2y. Accessed 9 June 2019.

Gabriel, Deborah. (2016). 'Blogging while Black, British and female: A critical study on discursive activism.' *Information, Communication & Society* 19(11): 1622–1635. https://doi.org/10.1080/1369118X.2016.1146784.

Gray, Kishonna L. (2015). 'Race, gender, and virtual inequality: Exploring the liberatory potential of Black cyberfeminist theory.' In *Produsing Theory in a Digital World 2.0: The Intersection of Audiences and Production in Contemporary Theory* Vol. 2, edited by Rebecca Ann Lind, pp. 175–192. New York: Peter Lang.

Hall, Stuart. (1993). 'Encoding, decoding.' In *The Cultural Studies Reader* (2nd ed.), edited by Simon During, pp. 507–517. London and New York: Routledge.

Hall, Stuart. (2003). 'The whites of their eyes: Racist ideologies and the media.' In *Gender, Race and Class in Media: A Text-Reader*, edited by Gail Dines & Jean M. Humez, pp. 89–93. Thousand Oaks, CA: Sage.

Hall, Stuart. (2018). Cited in *Uncut Funk: A Contemplative Dialogue*, written by bell hooks & Stuart Hall, p. 31. London: Routledge.

Harrison III, Robert L., Thomas, Kevin D. & Cross, Samantha N. N. (2015). 'Negotiating cultural ambiguity: The role of markets and consumption in multiracial identity development.' *Consumption Markets &*

Culture 18(4): 301–322. https://www.tandfonline.com/doi/abs/10.1080/10253866.2015.1019483?journalCode=gcmc20.

Hesmondhalgh, David & Saha, Anamik. (2013). 'Race, ethnicity, and cultural production.' *Popular Communication: The International Journal of Media and Culture* 11(3): 179–195. https://doi.org/10.1080/15405702.2013.810068.

Hobson, Janell. (2008). 'Digital whiteness, primitive blackness: Racializing the "digital divide" in film and new media.' *Feminist Media Studies* 8(2): 111–126. https://doi.org/10.1080/00220380801980467.

hooks, bell. (1992). *Black Looks: Race and Representation.* New York: Routledge.

hooks, bell. (1995). *Art on My Mind: Visual Politics.* New York: New Press.

hooks, bell. (2009). *Reel to Real: Race, Class and Sex at the Movies.* New York: Routledge.

hooks, bell. (2014). *Yearning: Race, Gender, and Cultural Politics* (2nd ed.). New York: Routledge.

hooks, bell. (2018). Cited in *Uncut Funk: A Contemplative Dialogue*, written by bell hooks & Stuart Hall, p. 6. London: Routledge.

Ibrahim, Yasmin. (2018). *Production of the 'Self' in the Digital Age.* Cham: Palgrave Macmillan.

Jackson, Sarah. J. (2016). '(Re)imagining intersectional democracy from Black feminism to hashtag activism.' *Women's Studies in Communication* 39(4): 375–379. https://doi.org/10.1080/07491409.2016.1226654.

Jarmon, Renina (@ReninaJarmon). (2013). *Black Girls Are From the Future: Essays On: Race, Digital Creativity and Pop Culture.* Washington, DC: Jarmon Media.

Johnson, Elizabeth. (2013). *Resistance and Empowerment in Black Women's Hair Styling.* Abingdon and New York: Routledge.

Johnson, Jessica Marie. (2018). 'Social stories: Digital storytelling and social media.' *Forum Journal* 32(1): 39–46. https://www.muse.jhu.edu/article/701681.

Jones, Feminista. (2019). *Reclaiming Our Space: How Black Feminists Are Changing the World from the Tweets to the Streets.* Boston: Beacon Press.

Joseph, Ralina L. (2012). *Transcending Blackness: From the New Millennium Mulatta to the Exceptional Multiracial.* Durham and London: Duke University.

Kolko, Beth E., Lisa, Nakamura & Rodman, Gilbert B. Rodman (eds.) (2000). *Race in Cyberspace.* New York and London: Routledge.

Lievrouw, Leah A. (2011). *Alternative and Activist New Media.* Cambridge and Malden, MA: Polity Press.

Lu, Jessica H. & Steele, Catherine Knight. (2019). '"Joy is resistance": Cross-platform resilience and (re)invention of Black oral culture online.' *Information, Communication & Society* 22(6): 823–837. https://doi.org/10.1080/1369118X.2019.1575449.

Makalani, Minkah. (2009). 'Introduction: Diaspora and the localities of race.' *Social Text* 27(98): 1–9. https://doi.org/10.1215/01642472-2008-014.

Maragh, Raven S. (2017). 'Authenticity on "Black Twitter": Reading racial performance and social networking.' *Television & New Media* 19(7): 591–609. https://doi.org/10.1177/1527476417738569.

McIlwain, Charlton. D. (2020). *Black Software: The Internet and Racial Justice, from the AfroNet to Black Lives Matter.* New York: Oxford University Press.

McMillan Cottom, Tressie. (2017). 'Black cyberfeminism: Ways forward for intersectionality and digital sociology.' In *Digital Sociologies*, edited by Jessie Daniels, Karen Gregory & Tressie McMillan Cottom, pp. 211–231. Bristol and Chicago: Policy Press.

Mohammed, Wunpini Fatimata. (2019). 'Online activism: Centering marginalized voices in activist work.' *Ada: A Journal of Gender, New Media & Technology* 15.https://adanewmedia.org/2019/02/issue15-mohammed.

Noble, Safiya Umoja. (2018). *Algorithms of Oppression: How Search Engines Reinforce Racism.* New York: New York University Press.

Noble, Safiya Umoja & Tynes, Brendesha M. (eds.) (2016). *The Intersectional Internet: Race, Sex, Class, and Culture Online.* New York: Peter Lang.

Nyabola, Nanjala. (2018). *Digital Democracy, Analogue Politics: How the Internet Era is Transforming Politics in Kenya.* London: Zed Books.

Osei, Krys. (2019). 'Fashioning my garden of solace: A Black feminist autoethnography.' *Fashion Theory* 23(6): 733–746. https://doi.org/10.1080/1362704X.2019.1657272.

Phelps-Ward, Robin J. & Laura, Crystal T. (2016). 'Talking back in cyberspace: Self-love, hair care, and counter narratives in Black adolescent girls' YouTube vlogs.' *Gender and Education* 28(6): 807–820. https://doi.org/10.1080/09540253.2016.1221888.

Saha, Anamik. (2012). 'Locating MIA: "race", commodification and the politics of production.' *European Journal of Cultural Studies* 15(6): 736–752. https://doi.org/10.1177/1367549412450633.

Sharma, Sanjay. (2013). 'Black Twitter? Racial hashtags, networks and contagion.' *New Formations* 78: 46–64. https://www.muse.jhu.edu/article/522093.

Sims, Jennifer Patrice & Njaka, Chinelo L. (2019). *Mixed-Race in the US and UK: Comparing the Past, Present, and Future.* Bingley: Emerald.

Sobande, Francesca. (2017). 'Watching me watching you: Black women in Britain on YouTube.' *European Journal of Cultural Studies* 20(6): 655–671. https://doi.org/10.1177/1367549417733001.

Sobande, Francesca, Fearfull, Anne & Brownlie, Douglas. (2019). 'Resisting media marginalisation: Black women's digital content and collectivity.' *Consumption Markets & Culture.* https://doi.org/10.1080/10253866.2019.1571491.

Sobande, Francesca & Osei, Krys. (2020). '*An African City*: Black women's creativity, pleasure, diasporic (dis)connections and resistance through aesthetic and media practices and scholarship.' *Communication, Culture & Critique*, tcz024. https://doi.org/10.1093/ccc/tcaa016.

Steele, Catherine Knight. (2016a). 'The digital barbershop: Blogs and online oral culture within the African American community.' *Social Media + Society* 2(4): 1–10. https://doi.org/10.1177/2056305116683205.

Steele, Catherine Knight. (2016b). 'Signifyin', bitching, and blogging: Black women and resistance discourse online.' In *The Intersectional Internet: Race, Sex, Class, and Culture Online*, edited by Safiya Umoja Noble & Brendesha M. Tynes, pp. 73–93. New York: Peter Lang.

Steele, Catherine Knight. (2017). 'Black bloggers and their varied publics: The everyday politics of black discourse online.' *Television & New Media* 19(2): 112–127. https://doi.org/10.1177/1527476417709535.

van Dijck, José. (2013). '"You have one identity": performing the self on Facebook and LinkedIn.' *Media, Culture & Society* 35(2): 199–215, https://doi.org/10.1177/0163443712468605.

Victoria, Stephanie. (2020). 'Grand opening. Grand closing. The life of #clubquarantine- and Black America.' *Medium.* Last modified 26 April, https://medium.com/@adreampreferredpodcast/grand-opening-grand-closing-the-life-of-clubquarantine-and-black-america-9caee13522b1. Accessed 1 May 2020.

Warner, Kristen J. (2015). 'ABC's *Scandal* and Black women's fandom.' In *Cupcakes, Pinterest and Ladyporn: Feminized Popular Culture in the Early Twenty-First Century*, edited by Elana Levine, pp. 32–50. Urbana, IL: University of Illinois Press.

Wheeler, André. (2019). 'Ten years of Black Twitter: A merciless watchdog for problematic behavior.' *The Guardian.* Last modified 23 December, https://www.theguardian.com/technology/2019/dec/23/ten-years-black-twitter-watchdog. Accessed 27 December 2019.

Open Access This chapter is licensed under the terms of the Creative Commons Attribution 4.0 International License (http://creativecommons.org/licenses/by/4.0/), which permits use, sharing, adaptation, distribution and reproduction in any medium or format, as long as you give appropriate credit to the original author(s) and the source, provide a link to the Creative Commons license and indicate if changes were made.

The images or other third party material in this chapter are included in the chapter's Creative Commons license, unless indicated otherwise in a credit line to the material. If material is not included in the chapter's Creative Commons license and your intended use is not permitted by statutory regulation or exceeds the permitted use, you will need to obtain permission directly from the copyright holder.

CHAPTER 5

(Un)Defining the Digital Lives of Black Women in Britain

Abstract This chapter is a closing consideration of why digital terrains continue to be a source of pleasure, creativity, and knowledge-sharing, as well as distress and danger for Black women in Britain. It reflects on the (un)definable nature of the digital experiences of Black women in Britain, similarities and differences between them, and the impact of the COVID-19 (coronavirus) global pandemic in 2020.

Keywords Black Women · Britain · COVID-19 · Digital · Internet · Representation

The digital experiences of Black women in Britain take many different forms. For some, they are mostly filled with conversations with online and 'IRL' friends, types of creativity, and Black diasporic knowledge-sharing. For others, misogynoir (Bailey 2010; Bailey and Trudy 2018) and the entanglements of intersecting oppressions mar their online encounters in ways that are extremely harmful to them (Akiwowo 2018; Allman 2019). For many Black women in Britain their digital experiences may oscillate between the joy, play, ingenuity, and resistance that can be involved in their use of the internet—such as when communicating and collaborating with other Black people, and participating in spaces such as Black Twitter

© The Author(s) 2020
F. Sobande, *The Digital Lives of Black Women in Britain*,
Palgrave Studies in (Re)Presenting Gender,
https://doi.org/10.1007/978-3-030-46679-4_5

(Brock 2020; Chatman 2017; Clark 2014; Lu and Steele 2019; Shand-Baptiste 2020; Wheeler 2019)—while also dealing with danger, trauma, abuse, and violence linked to white supremacist digital activity, among other malicious entities (Daniels 2009, 2012, 2017; Lewis 2018; Palmer 2019).

The digital encounters of Black women in Britain can entail forging and feeling part of a collective experience or preferring to create a low-key and anonymous presence that enables them to quietly observe activities, interactions, and movements within digital spaces. Such digital experiences can involve intentional forms of entrepreneurialism and work, as well as efforts to share educational and marketplace advice that is tailored to Black women (Croxford 2018; Gabriel 2016; Sobande 2017; Sobande et al. 2019; Wilson-Ojo 2017). Further still, the digital experiences of Black women in Britain—regardless of their potential transience—are always shaped by specific and tangible spaces, including the intricacies of different geo-cultural contexts and types of regionality and rurality.

The extent to which digital media and the internet play a central role in the lives of such women can considerably vary, including due to generational, socio-economic, and location-based differences which should not be overlooked. Furthermore, '[t]echnological innovation promises to improve our lives, but there is always a chasm between our aspirations and reality' (Daniels et al. 2019, p. 3). As the childhood experiences of Bobino highlight, a consistent supply of electricity in a household is far from being the norm for all Black girls and women in Britain, nor is constant access to the internet, a computer, laptop, mobile phone, or television.

Although my book undeniably focuses on the digital encounters of Black women in Britain, it would be inaccurate to paint a picture which implies that all Black women have equal access to the internet, online activities, and devices through which they can create, post, curate, share, and respond to digital content. In addition, having access to such resources should not be uncritically equated with being able to have some form of power, visible digital presence, or the ability to easily and often participate in digital discussions (Gray 2015).

Right now—late March 2020—as the COVID-19 (coronavirus) global pandemic grips populations, places, and politics around the world, the role of digital media and digital culture in the daily lives of many is heightened. The pandemic emerged during the final weeks of writing this book.

I found myself having to figure out how to mourn a loss through communion at a distance with family members over video calls, and through sharing photographs in digital albums that brought joy, peace, and a sense of intimacy during a time when physical social connection and gathering was not possible. I felt the warmth of friendships that I am eternally thankful for in the form of conversations that quickly morph from the sharing of funny memes to long audio messages, followed by hours of speaking on the phone. During this time, for some individuals who have relatively consistent access to the internet and devices that enable them to connect with others online, digital spaces and networked communities may be their prime, or, even, sole, source of social interaction for the foreseeable future.

For some Black women in Britain, including those who actively avoid certain digital technologies and social media sites, the societal emphasis on digital connectivity and online sociality that has been exacerbated amid this time of crisis may result in them being encouraged—and, even, directed—to use and participate in digital spaces against their wishes, and which pose great risks to their safety, privacy, health, and wellbeing. Moreover, for Black women in Britain who cannot access such technologies and digital spaces, the pronounced societal emphasis on digital communication at present, alongside the absence of the availability of free broadband for all, and the extremely limited nature of support that is not distinctly linked to digital communication, may be preventing them from accessing vital information, help, and services.

Acknowledging the digital difficulties and dilemmas yielded by societal responses to COVID-19 is not to dismiss the fact that many connected digital issues existed before. However, the ability of Black women to exert their agency and exercise a certain amount of choice and control over some of their digital experiences may be especially constrained in this specific moment—when institutions, such as governmental ones, employers, commercial organisations, and even some non-profits, may be punitively instructing Black women to go online in order to access crucial information that they require, or to communicate with organisations and carry out tasks that are in the interest of institutions but hinder the safety, privacy, health, and wellbeing of Black women.

The impact of COVID-19 on life as 'we' know it will no doubt be examined in detail in the weeks, months, and years that follow. Hopefully related writing, work, and discussion will account for how in addition to digital technology facilitating sociality and aiding a sense of connection between people and places in ways that are enriching to them, digital technology and its significant role in the daily lives of many—including as ordered by institutions—was and is weaponised against some people.

Since the COVID-19 global pandemic has rapidly expanded and the number of people staying at home for long periods of time has increased, there have been numerous cases of white supremacist, far-right, and misogynistic groups targeting Black women and attempting to disrupt their work and online interactions—such as by entering video conferencing spaces via Zoom, where Black women have been bombarded with abuse. There are countless examples of how the ill-considered 'pivot to online' approach of many institutions is amplifying various risks that people are exposed to, including the targeted trolling that often accompanies the visibility of Black women online—some of whom are navigating an increased pressure to participate and present themselves in different digital spaces where they may be harassed and harmed.

As I attempt to make sense of what is happening around the world and how it is affecting Black women, while being cognisant of my limited understanding and geo-culturally specific perspective, I remain conscious of the potential to overestimate the extent to which Black women's digital experiences are changing right now. After all, Black women have faced a lot of targeted harassment and abuse online, long before COVID-19. However, I am acutely aware that many aspects of the lives of Black women in Britain *have* changed during this time, including their digital experiences—often out of necessity—and sometimes as a result of employers' and capitalist institutions' efforts to maintain productivity and profit by attempting to force individuals to maximise the use of digital technology and participate in digital communication that enables harmful entities to surveil Black women.

'[R]aced and gendered subjects, constructed in the realm of digital media and technology, suggest that the power dynamics that exist offline get reproduced online in dominant media in disturbing and retrogressive ways' (Hobson 2008, p. 112). For many reasons—including safety concerns and a lack of access which is shaped by the intersections of anti-Black racism, sexism, classism, and ableism—Black women in Britain may not be able to take part in, and may actively avoid, various digital experiences. Thus, despite *The Digital Lives of Black Women in Britain* being a book that foregrounds precisely what the title suggests, it was written with an understanding of the reality that the internet, social media, online content-sharing platforms, and digital discourse do not play a significant role in the lives of all Black women in Britain, and are experienced by Black women in many different ways.

As well as 'the myth of a single narrative of Blackness' (Lu and Steele 2019, p. 831) that circulates in societies, there is sometimes an associated myth of a singular homogenous Black digital experience. While my book discusses similarities between some of the digital experiences of Black women in Britain, it also includes recognition of differences which counter essentialising notions of what it means to be a Black woman in Britain today, and to experience the internet. Just as 'the personal is the political' (Wilson cited in the Brixton Black Women's Group & the Organisation for Women of African and Asian Descent 2017, p. 3), both the personal and the political are sometimes digital. The digital experiences of Black women in Britain can involve speaking up about, bearing witness to, and challenging various socio-political issues. At times, it is by turning to social media that Black women campaign for change, lead, and contribute to collective attempts to push against white supremacist capitalist patriarchy—in ways that strengthen connected offline activism rather than replace it (Jackson et al. 2020).

The digital encounters of many who I interviewed exemplify 'the central work that Black women take on as part of the interactive economy of media (television and Twitter)' (Maragh 2016, p. 353). Some of the women who I interviewed discussed feeling pressures to constantly present themselves and have something to say online, as well as sharing concerns about the potential for a societal focus on what people say and do online, to eclipse and erase what people are saying and doing and have already said and done, offline. In other words: 'If a tree falls and there's nobody there to tweet about it, did it happen?'

Despite there being commonalities between the digital experiences of Black women in Britain, alike the lives that these experiences are a part of, there are also many differences between them—including due to the prevalence of interrelated ableism, classism, colourism, homophobia, Islamophobia, transphobia, xenophobia, and other types of intermingled structural oppression. Returning once more to the words of Beverley Bryan et al. (2018, p. 2) on the lives of Black women in Britain:

> If we are to gain anything from our history and from our lives in this country which can be of practical use to us today, we must take stock of our experiences, assess our responses – and learn from them.

The narratives of Black women which are reflected in my book speak to some of the specific ways that Black women in Britain experience the internet, social media, and learn from the digital encounters of others. The interviews that underpin much of this writing signal that digital spaces, platforms, and communication channels have contributed to how the work of Black women in Britain is documented and distributed—but sometimes in ways that can result in it being commodified and co-opted. Although nobody's safety or privacy online can be guaranteed, the precarious and simultaneously invisible and hyper-visible position that Black women in Britain may find themselves in is irrefutably affected by the particularities of misogynoir (Bailey 2010; Bailey and Trudy 2018) and a matrix of oppression (Hill Collins 2000).

For some of the Black women who I spoke to, their creation of digital content and sharing of writing online was primarily motivated by an intention to produce freely accessible resources that could benefit other Black women. As such, they were disinterested in notions of ownership and credit for their content which they felt were inherently linked to capitalistic concepts of value and individualistic notions of property and possession. For others, they sought to produce and share knowledge in non-hierarchical ways which they felt were outside of the confines of elitist and exclusionary institutions, but while also ensuring that they were fairly paid for such work. Questions concerning 'Intellectual property vs. free culture' (Wong 2017, p. 204) were often considered as part of their creation of digital content, especially if they were self-employed creative and cultural workers.

Certain digital spaces present the potential for Black people around the world to depict themselves, record their histories, and steer public discourse about their own identities and communities, but, while often finding that in doing so, their digital discussions may be (re)used and (re)presented in ways that serve others' commercial interests. Put briefly, even if the digital experiences and activities of some Black women in Britain involve them upholding an anti-capitalist position, social media, digital spaces, and much of the broader society that they are a part of does not exist outside of the strictures of capitalism. Therefore, the digital experiences of Black women—and their marketplace participation in general—can involve traversing tensions between their personal principles and the commercial values of institutions, such as, for some, disconnections between their resistant political position and the inescapably capitalist and oppressive makeup of various environments and organisations that they inevitably encounter or exist within.

In 2009, film and media studies scholar Anna Everett observed that 'it appears that computer-mediated communication (CMC) is refashioning the concept and utility of a viable black public sphere in the new millennium' (p. 14). Continued digital advancements have expanded the ways that Black women in Britain are depicted in media, including how they produce and share content themselves. Although in recent years there has been an indication of media depictions of Black women changing, since the release of early filmic images, Black women continue to be represented in media in derogatory ways. Some of the means through which such media portrayals are transmitted have changed with the advent of social media. Yet, many discriminatory ideas about Black women and disparaging images of them have stubbornly stayed the same.

As I maintain throughout this book, the term 'representation matters' often functions in meaningless ways—especially when stripped of any scrutiny of connected material conditions, work and labour experiences, media production processes and who is involved in them, and prevailing structural inequalities. Nevertheless, as visual cultures and media depictions within them remain societally influential, it can be misguided to entirely disregard what media representations and how they do (not) change suggest about socio-political issues and struggles. More specifically, examining media representations in tandem with robust critique of the material realities that propel them and which they reflect and reframe, can be one of, or, part of, many effective means of examining past and contemporary hierarchical dynamics—such as who has power and control over media production processes and how this is made manifest in media depictions.

Celebratory comments concerning perceived increases in the representation of Black women in media in Britain are often based on the mistaken assumption that any rising frequency of how often they feature in the media indicates their improved treatment in society and dismantling of oppressive structures that hamper their lives. However, representation in 'an economy of visibility' (Banet-Weiser 2018, p. 2) should not be confused for substantial types of structural action, especially as corporations continue to vociferously 'capitalize on calls for diversity' (Benjamin 2019, p. 18). Besides, when reflecting on any changes to the visibility of Black women in the media in Britain there is a need to critically consider which Black women are (not) being depicted? How are they being depicted? Who is depicting them, narrating their depiction, and with what intention? Where are they depicted? Who is the (un)intended audience? What messages and meanings may be encoded and decoded (Hall 1993)?

Symbols and signifiers associated with Black culture and Black women's physical embodiment continue to be linked to cultural cachet and coolness, but especially when expressed and appropriated by people who are not Black (Jackson 2019). As a result, the digital discourse and depictions that Black women in Britain construct and communicate are highly susceptible to being decontextualised, recontextualised, repurposed, and repackaged by watchful dominant social groups and marketplace institutions—including mainstream media organisations that 'in their haste to keep pace with viral and innovative social media content created by relatively unknown online-users…frequently (mis)use individuals' digital content' (Sobande 2019, p. 156). As the digital presence and cultural production of Black women in Britain continues to gain the attention of expansive audiences and organisations, it is important to critically question the intentions of those that profess to support Black women.

Recognising tensions between the countercultural, communal, and commercial qualities of digital spaces and online sites, this book examines how the intersections of anti-Black racism, sexism, and capitalism are connected to Black women's digital encounters, as well as linked material conditions, marketplace contexts, and structural inequalities. The experiences considered in my book highlight Black women's construction and sharing of culturally specific knowledge in digital spaces and as part of the transmission of Black diasporic insight, including via production and spectatorship of media. Many of such experiences are examples of Black women's 'harnessing of the democratizing possibilities of postindustrial society's rapidly congealing information technocracy' (Everett 2009, p. 14). As the digital presence of Black women in Britain can involve them encountering abuse, harassment, and numerous risks, many face navigating often discriminatory digital terrains, but still persist and seek out different digital experiences—including to share resources with each other, work together, have fun, pass time, express themselves, and, for some, co-create in a manner that resists neoliberal and hyper-competitive market logics.

The agency and creativity of many of such women is not up for debate. There are numerous examples of how Black women in Britain are using digital tools and technologies as part of counter-cultural commitments to challenge dominant structures and to create content that is absent in more mainstream and formal media and educational contexts, as well as copious examples of such individuals using digital spaces to share art and support the creative practice of other Black women. For some Black women in Britain, it is through pockets of the internet and social media that their Black feminist principles and work have developed, but the politics of Black women can drastically differ from one another, and resistant and counter-hegemonic intentions, in addition to a so-called 'leftist' or 'radical' ideological point of view, should not be assumed. Thus, it is important to recognise that the digital experiences of some Black women in Britain may be at odds with those of others.

No one Black woman's digital presence, perspective, and politics should be mistaken for representing a unified, unchanging, and collective point of view of all Black women. Still, the burden of representation continues to weigh heavily on Black women in Britain, particularly when their digital presence becomes increasingly public and high-profile— potentially leading to people portraying them as a spokesperson for all Black women. Over the years, I have lost count of the number of times I have witnessed people indignantly demand the time, comments, engagement, work, and labour of Black women on social media. The digital hyper-visibility of some such women can often be accompanied by other people's disrespectful sense of entitlement regarding access to Black women's thoughts, work, and personal space—in ways which are impacted by colourism, and reflect dominant societal expectations that Black women's lives are anchored in working in the service of others (Bryan et al. 2018).

What will the future hold for the digital lives of Black women in Britain? When considering this it is necessary 'to take time out to appreciate our past and thus better prepare the way forward' (Wilson 1982, p. 31). As I write this, some Black women in Britain are signing into social media accounts, while others may be signing out, for good. Some may have always lived a life free of social media, while others find that such digital spaces and online connections are enriching in ways that once seemed unimaginable. Some may question the capacity to find and create communities online, while others may beg to differ. Some may view their digital experiences as being spurred on by social justice and Black feminist aims, while others think of theirs as being far from political.

The digital experiences of Black women in Britain take many different forms—archiving, self-documenting, storytelling, poetry-making, collaborating, producing, pausing, speaking, sharing, anticipating, theorising, responding, agitating, caring, enjoying, retreating, resisting, reading, and reflecting. Such experiences are messy, ever-changing, (un)definable, (un)comfortable, creative, and can be an (un)equal source of pleasure, play, and pedagogy, as well as pressure, peril, and pain.

References

Akiwowo, Seyi. (2018). 'Amnesty's latest research into online abuse finally confirms what Black women have known for over a decade.' *Huffington Post.* Last modified 19 December, https://www.huffingtonpost.co.uk/entry/amnesty-online-abuse-women-twitter_uk_5c1a0a2fe4b02d2cae8ea0c1. Accessed 17 January 2019.

Allman, Esme. (2019). 'The dark side of social media for Black women.' *Black Ballad.* Last modified 14 February, https://blackballad.co.uk/people/the-dark-side-of-social-media-for-black-women?listIds=5d93b25a88157fff350b6d2e. Accessed 20 February 2019.

Bailey, Moya. (2010). 'They aren't talking about me ...' *Crunk Feminist Collective.* Last modified 14 March, http://www.crunkfeministcollective.com/2010/03/14/they-arent-talking-about-me/. Accessed 28 March 2020.

Bailey, Moya & Trudy. (2018). 'On misogynoir: citation, erasure, and plagiarism.' *Feminist Media Studies* 18(4): 762–768. https://doi.org/10.1080/14680777.2018.1447395.

Banet-Weiser, Sarah. (2018). *Empowered: Popular Feminism and Popular Misogyny.* Durham and London: Duke University Press.

Benjamin, Ruha. (2019). *Race After Technology: Abolitionist Tools for the New Jim Code.* Cambridge and Medford, MA: Polity Press.

Brock, André. (2020). *Distributed Blackness: African American Cybercultures.* New York: New York University Press.

Bryan, Beverley, Dadzie, Stella & Scafe, Suzanne. (2018). *The Heart of the Race: Black Women's Lives in Britain* (2nd ed.). London: Verso.

Chatman, Dayna. (2017). 'Black Twitter and the politics of viewing Scandal.' In *Fandom: Identities and Communities in a Mediated World* (2nd ed.), edited by Jonathan Gray, Cornel Sandvoss & C. Lee Harrington, pp. 299–314. New York: New York University.

Clark, Meredith D. (2014). 'To tweet our own cause: A mixed-methods study of the online phenomenon "Black Twitter".' Chapel Hill, NC: University of

North Carolina at Chapel Hill Graduate School, 2014. https://doi.org/10.17615/7bfs-rp55.

Croxford, Rianna. (2018). 'What it is like for a black student to go to Cambridge.' *Financial Times.* Last modified 31 May 2018, https://www.ft.com/content/cad952d2-215d-11e8-8d6c-a1920d9e946f. Accessed 2 June 2018.

Daniels, Jessie. (2009). *Cyber Racism: White Supremacy Online and the New Attack on Civil Rights.* New York: Rowman & Littlefield.

Daniels, Jessie. (2012). 'Race and racism in Internet studies: A review and critique.' *New Media & Society* 15(5): 695–719. https://doi.org/10.1177/1461444812462849.

Daniels, Jessie. (2017). 'Twitter and white supremacy, a love story.' *DAME Magazine.* Last modified 19 October, https://www.damemagazine.com/2017/10/19/twitter-and-white-supremacy-love-story. Accessed 10 July 2019.

Daniels, Jessie, Nkonde, Mutale & Mir, Darakhshan. (2019). 'Advancing racial literacy in tech: Why ethics, diversity in hiring & implicit bias trainings aren't enough.' *Data & Society.* Last modified May 2019, https://datasociety.net/wp-content/uploads/2019/05/Racial_Literacy_Tech_Final_0522.pdf. Accessed 15 February 2020.

Everett, Anna. (2009). *Digital Diaspora: A Race for Cyberspace.* Albany, NY: SUNY Press.

Gabriel, Deborah. (2016). 'Blogging while Black, British and female: A critical study on discursive activism.' *Information, Communication & Society* 19(11): 1622–1635. https://doi.org/10.1080/1369118X.2016.1146784.

Gray, Kishonna L. (2015). 'Race, gender, and virtual inequality: Exploring the liberatory potential of Black cyberfeminist theory.' In *Producing Theory in a Digital World 2.0: The Intersection of Audiences and Production in Contemporary Theory* Vol. 2, edited by Rebecca Ann Lind, pp. 175–192. New York: Peter Lang.

Hall, Stuart. (1993). 'Encoding, decoding.' In *The Cultural Studies Reader* (2nd ed.), edited by Simon During, pp. 507–517. London and New York: Routledge.

Hill Collins, Patricia. (2000). *Black Feminist Thought: Knowledge, Consciousness, and the Politics of Empowerment* (2nd ed.). New York and London: Routledge.

Hobson, Janell. (2008). 'Digital whiteness, primitive blackness: Racializing the "digital divide" in film and new media.' *Feminist Media Studies* 8(2): 111–126. https://doi.org/10.1080/00220380801980467.

Jackson, Lauren Michele. (2019). *White Negroes: When Cornrows Were in Vogue … and Other Thoughts on Cultural Appropriation.* Boston: Beacon Press.

Jackson, Sarah J., Bailey, Moya & Foucault Welles, Brooke. (2020). *#HashtagActivism: Networks of Race and Gender Justice*. Cambridge, MA and London: MIT Press.

Lewis, Rebecca. (2018). 'Alternative influence: Broadcasting the reactionary right on YouTube.' *Data & Society*, https://datasociety.net/wp-content/uploads/2018/09/DS_Alternative_Influence.pdf. Accessed 15 March 2019.

Lu, Jessica H. & Steele, Catherine Knight. (2019). '"Joy is resistance": Cross-platform resilience and (re)invention of Black oral culture online.' *Information, Communication & Society* 22(6): 823–837. https://doi.org/10.1080/1369118X.2019.1575449.

Maragh, Raven S. (2016). '"Our struggles are unequal": Black women's affective labor between television and Twitter.' *Journal of Communication Inquiry* 40(4): 351–369. https://doi.org/10.1177/0196859916664082.

Palmer, Lisa Amanda. (2019). 'Diane Abbott, misogynoir and the politics of Black British feminism's anticolonial imperatives: "In Britain too, it's as if we don't exist".' *The Sociological Review*. https://doi.org/10.1177/0038026119892404.

Shand-Baptiste, Kuba. 2020. 'The viral stars of Black Twitter are finally being recognised—and that's worth celebrating.' *The Independent*. Last modified 1 January, https://www.independent.co.uk/voices/black-twitter-memes-instagram-kayla-nicole-jones-anthony-spice-adams-antoine-dodson-a9266721.html Accessed 2 January 2020.

Sobande, Francesca. (2017). 'Watching me watching you: Black women in Britain on YouTube.' *European Journal of Cultural Studies* 20(6): 655–671. https://doi.org/10.1177/1367549417733001.

Sobande, Francesca. (2019). 'Memes, digital remix culture and (re)mediating British politics and public life.' *IPPR Progressive Review* 26(2): 151–160. https://doi.org/10.1111/newe.12155.

Sobande, Francesca, Fearfull, Anne & Brownlie, Douglas. (2019). 'Resisting media marginalisation: Black women's digital content and collectivity.' *Consumption Markets & Culture*, https://doi.org/10.1080/10253866.2019.1571491.

Wheeler, André (2019). 'Ten years of Black Twitter: A merciless watchdog for problematic behavior.' *The Guardian*. Last modified 23 December, https://www.theguardian.com/technology/2019/dec/23/ten-years-black-twitter-watchdog. Accessed 27 December 2019.

Wilson, Melba. (1982). 'Black Women Writers.' *Spare Rib* 119: 31–32.

Wilson, Melba. (2017). Cited in *Black Women Organising*, written by the Brixton Black Women's Group and the Organisation for Women of African and Asian Descent, p. 3 London: past tense.

Wilson-Ojo, Madeline. (2017). 'Social media has done for Black British women in one decade what TV couldn't in thirty years.' *The Huffington Post*. Last modified 17 December, https://www.huffingtonpost.co.uk/entry/black-women-social-media_uk_5a36b3d2e4b0e7f1200cfc1b. Accessed 20 December 2017.

Wong, Ashley Lee. (2017). 'Work in the creative economy: Living contradictions between the market and creative collaboration.' In *Collaborative Production in the Creative Industries*, edited by James Graham & Alessandro Gandini, pp. 197–215. London: University of Westminster Press.

Index

A

Activism, 4, 12, 14, 34, 38, 89, 117, 123, 135
activist, 6, 11, 14, 34, 37, 38, 43, 44, 68, 72, 73, 90, 115, 119. *See also* Black feminism, Black feminist
Africa/n, 3, 11, 14, 19, 30–32, 35, 49, 55, 77, 78, 91, 115, 118, 121, 135
African American, 4, 39, 44, 46, 102, 103, 109
Algorithm, 12, 44, 80. *See also* Noble, Safiya Umoja
Anti-Black/ness, 1, 3, 4, 9, 14, 19, 30, 32, 34–36, 39, 40, 42–45, 47, 51, 54, 55, 72, 75, 76, 83, 86, 88, 89, 91, 102, 105, 110, 115, 121, 134, 138
Archive/ing, 11, 31, 73, 140
Artist/s, 6, 11, 14, 34, 46, 47, 73, 79, 82, 102, 112, 116

B

Bailey, Moya, 14, 43, 44, 72, 74, 76, 131, 136. *See also* Hashtag; Misogynoir
Benjamin, Ionie, 66, 72. *See also* Black press
Benjamin, Ruha, 5, 8, 12, 39, 88, 102, 137
Bishop, Marla, 34
Black art/ist, 66, 81, 82, 88
Black British, 5, 42, 46, 73, 105, 120
Black Cultural Archives (BCA), 15, 31
Black cyberfeminism, 13, 89
   Black cyberfeminist, 13, 86. *See also* Gray, Kishonna L.; McMillan Cottom, Tressie
Black feminism, 14, 30, 34, 90
   Black feminist, 4, 6, 11, 13, 44, 68, 90. *See also* Brixton Black Women's Group; Bryan, Beverley; Dadzie, Stella; Emejulu, Akwugo; Hill Collins, Patricia; hooks, bell; Lewis,

Gail; Scafe, Suzanne; *The Heart of The Race: Black Women's Lives in Britain*
Black girl/s, 3, 10, 46, 48, 53, 116, 122, 132
Black press, 72. See also Benjamin, Ionie
Black Twitter, 76, 90, 109, 124, 129. See also Brock, André; Clark, Meredith D.
Blog/ging, 18, 73. See also Gabriel, Deborah; Steele, Catherine Knight
Bobo, Jacqueline, 13, 42, 44, 111, 116, 119, 121
Brand/s, 42, 70, 80, 84, 87–89, 112
Brexit, 30
Brixton Black Women's Group, 11, 14, 30, 32, 135
Brock, André, 5, 10, 78, 102, 132. See also Black Twitter
Bruce, Keisha, 5, 6
Bryan, Beverley, 2, 4, 11, 12, 30, 31, 34, 35, 43, 53, 68, 135, 139. See also Black feminism, Black feminist; *The Heart of The Race: Black Women's Lives in Britain*
Business, 16, 77, 88, 103, 107, 122

C

Capitalism, 1, 3, 10, 43, 67, 68, 71, 120, 123, 136, 138
  capitalist/ic, 3, 14, 18, 35, 70, 79, 84, 123, 134–137
Cardiff, 53
Caribbean, 19, 31, 35
Clark, Meredith D., 5, 6, 10, 78, 83, 102, 109
Class/ism, 4, 8, 30, 32, 34, 39, 55, 66–68, 71, 75, 76, 88, 89, 115, 118, 134, 135

Collective/ly, 6, 8, 17, 31–34, 38, 50, 54, 68, 74, 79, 81, 91, 102, 110, 111, 116, 120, 123, 132, 135, 139
Colourism, 8, 9, 40, 47, 51, 74, 76, 107, 135, 139
  shadeism, 9
Commodification, 78, 116, 122
  commodify, 91. See also Consumer culture
Consciousness-raising, 14, 34, 50, 73
Consumer culture, 10, 38, 42, 69, 90, 123. See also Commodification, commodify
COVID-19, 11, 18, 69, 132–134
Creative/ly, 3, 11, 13, 16, 18, 30–34, 38, 41, 43, 44, 50, 51, 53, 54, 66, 67, 70–73, 75–85, 87–91, 120, 123, 136, 139, 140
  creativity, 1, 6, 12, 19, 50, 52, 66, 67, 71, 72, 74, 75, 77, 81, 84, 85, 87, 89–91, 102, 131, 139
Cultural industry/ies, 18, 38, 41, 66, 79, 81, 89, 91
Cultural production, 1, 3, 6, 67, 71, 72, 90, 122, 138

D

Dadzie, Stella, 2, 11, 12, 68, 135. See Black feminism, Black feminist; *The Heart of The Race: Black Women's Lives in Britain*
Daniels, Jessie, 4, 18, 80, 132
Dating, 113, 114
Decolonise, 80, 117. See also Owusu, Melz
Diaspora, 8, 104, 105, 121
Digital Blackness, 5, 103, 104, 106
Digital culture, 4, 10, 18, 37, 38, 75, 85, 111, 132
Digital diaspora, 6, 9, 101, 112, 122, 138. See also Everett, Anna

Digital remix culture, 17, 38, 39, 70
Digital studies, 2–4, 6, 13, 102
Digital technology, 13, 16, 36, 75, 78, 89, 102, 104, 133, 134

E
Edinburgh, 34
Education/al, 4, 11, 16, 32, 44, 66, 71, 77, 88, 90, 116, 132, 139
Emejulu, Akwugo, 4, 8, 9, 13, 30, 35, 90, 103, 118. *See also* Black feminism, Black feminist
Employment, 51, 68, 69. *See also* Labour
England, 7, 12, 13, 41, 46, 48, 50, 53, 55, 73–75, 77, 80, 107, 109, 113, 116, 119
English, 5, 7, 9, 107
Everett, Anna, 2, 5, 6, 9, 10, 66, 78, 102, 107, 112, 121, 122, 137, 138. *See also* Digital diaspora

F
Facebook, 2, 36, 74, 80, 105, 107, 113
Film/ic, 6, 34, 45, 50, 53, 75, 102, 116, 121, 137
Friend/s, 2, 14, 40, 46, 48, 50, 74, 86, 114, 115, 122, 131

G
Gabriel, Deborah, 3, 6, 9, 38, 42, 51, 66, 73, 74, 102, 132. *See also* Blog/ging
Gaze, 16, 44, 84
Gender, 3, 4, 8, 10, 13, 14, 18, 32, 38–41, 55, 71, 75, 76, 85, 89, 102, 107
Girl/s, 3, 33, 46, 113
Glasgow, 53

Gray, Kishonna L., 5, 13, 38, 66, 75, 76, 85, 86, 102. *See also* Black cyberfeminism, Black cyberfeminist

H
Hair, 18, 76, 111–113, 115, 116, 122
Hall, Stuart, 31, 37, 107, 117, 121. *See also* Representation
Harassment, 3, 14, 37, 41, 55, 74, 76, 77, 84–86, 134, 138
Hashtag, 43, 101, 102
Health, 30, 32, 36, 37, 86, 90, 133
The Heart of The Race: Black Women's Lives in Britain, 11, 35. *See also* Black feminism, Black feminist; Bryan, Beverley; Dadzie, Stella; Scafe, Suzanne
Heteronormative, 42, 43, 47, 106, 119
Hill Collins, Patricia, 4, 9, 17, 30, 44, 45, 54, 67, 84, 136. *See also* Black feminism, Black feminist
hill, layla-roxanne, 6, 7, 34, 42, 52, 79, 89, 90. *See also* Scotland
hooks, bell, 43–45, 68, 69, 107, 119, 120, 122. *See also* Black feminism, Black feminist

I
Ideology/cal, 41–45, 49, 51, 76, 108, 112, 117, 120, 139
Influencer, 16, 70, 80
Instagram, 2, 36, 83, 84, 87, 105
Intersecting oppressions, 14, 30, 44, 51, 83, 89, 131
 intersecting inequalities, 17, 33
Islamophobia, 39, 40, 54, 76, 135

J

Jackson, Sarah J., 5, 43, 79, 102, 135, 138. *See also* Hashtag
Johnson, Azeezat, 4, 39
Jokes, 47

K

Knowledge-production, 72, 89, 114
knowledge-sharing, 18, 19, 67, 72, 110, 114, 131

L

Labour, 9, 32, 35, 43, 67–70, 137, 139. *See also* Employment
Lewis, Gail, 4, 11, 14, 30, 31, 68, 80. *See also* Black feminism, Black feminist; Brixton Black Women's Group
Liverpool, 53

M

Marketing, 13, 16, 38, 73, 77, 79, 84. *See also* Brand/s; Commodification; Consumer Culture; Marketplace
Marketplace, 4, 10, 13, 14, 38, 43, 49, 50, 52, 67, 70, 71, 90, 91, 123, 132, 136, 138
McMillan Cottom, Tressie, 4, 5, 13, 84, 86, 102. *See also* Black cyberfeminism, Black cyberfeminist
(Medi)activist, 117–119, 123
Misogynoir, 14, 72, 74, 76, 86, 102, 131. *See also* Bailey, Moya; Trudy

N

Noble, Safiya Umoja, 5, 12, 17, 44, 80, 102. *See also* Algorithm

Northern Ireland, 7, 13, 53, 106
Not-for-profit, 86
non-profit, 73, 133

O

Organisation for Women of African and Asian Descent, 30
Owusu, Melz, 6, 31. *See also* Decolonise

P

Politics, 12, 18, 30, 32, 36–39, 42, 45, 52, 67, 71, 72, 82, 83, 89, 90, 103–109, 132, 139
Power, 12, 13, 17, 30, 36, 43, 44, 67, 71, 76, 79, 81, 90, 104–106, 111, 123, 132, 134, 137
Profit/able, 67, 70, 78, 79, 84, 134

Q

Queer, 47, 55, 119

R

Regional/ity, 7, 18, 34, 41, 45, 49, 52, 53, 77, 89, 106, 107, 132
Representation, 4, 13, 18, 35, 37–39, 41–44, 46, 49–53, 82, 89, 90, 106, 116, 121, 137, 139
Resist/ance, 6, 11, 13, 16, 18, 32, 37, 38, 43, 68, 69, 77, 78, 85, 89–91, 102, 117–119, 123, 137, 139, 140
Rural/ity, 8, 18, 53, 132

S

Scafe, Suzanne, 2, 11, 12, 68, 135. *See also The Heart of The Race: Black Women's Lives in Britain*

Scotland, 7, 12, 13, 34, 40, 41, 47–49, 51–53, 55, 79, 106, 109, 111, 112, 114–116, 118, 121
Scottish, 7, 41, 52, 53
Sexuality, 8, 14, 39, 76, 102, 107
Spare Rib, 33, 34, 37, 66, 83, 90
Steele, Catherine Knight, 5, 6, 74, 78, 102, 110. *See* Blog/ging
Sulter, Maud, 7, 11, 30, 66

T
Teach, 71
Television, 2, 4, 18, 38, 45–48, 51, 53, 54, 85, 111, 115, 118–120, 122, 132, 135
TikTok, 2, 84
Transphobia, 32, 43, 76, 83, 135
Trouble, 2, 46–49, 87, 103
Trudy, 14, 72, 74, 76, 131, 136. *See also* Misogynoir

V
Video, 15, 18, 33, 52, 53, 70, 76, 77, 84, 86, 91, 111, 115, 119, 121, 122, 133, 134
Vine, 76, 91
Viral, 37, 38, 91, 138
Vlog/ger, 18, 73, 76, 77, 103, 111–122. *See also* YouTube

W
Walcott, Rianna, 5, 6, 30, 31
Wales, 7, 12, 13, 53
Welsh, 7
Wilson, Melba, 14, 29, 32, 135, 139

Y
YouTube, 2, 4, 17, 18, 36, 74, 76, 77, 90, 105, 110–122. *See also* Vlog/ger

The manufacturer's authorised representative in the EU is Springer Nature Customer Service Centre GmbH, Europaplatz 3, 69115 Heidelberg, Germany. If you have any concerns regarding our products, please contact ProductSafety@springernature.com

Printed and bound by CPI Group (UK) Ltd, Croydon, CR0 4YY

25/03/2026

02078205-0009